Jewish
Fairy Tales

Jewish Fairy Tales

GERALD FRIEDLANDER

DOVER PUBLICATIONS, INC.
Mineola, New York

DOVER JUVENILE CLASSICS

EDITOR OF THIS VOLUME: JANET BAINE KOPITO

Published in Canada by General Publishing Company, Ltd., 895 Don Mills Road, 400-2 Park Centre, Toronto, Ontario M3C 1W3.

Published in the United Kingdom by David & Charles, Brunel House, Forde Close, Newton Abbot, Devon TQ12 4PU.

Bibliographical Note

This Dover edition of *Jewish Fairy Tales,* first published in 2001, is an unabridged republication of *The Jewish Fairy Book,* originally published by Frederick A. Stokes Company, New York, in 1920.

Library of Congress Cataloging-in-Publication Data

Friedlander, Gerald, 1871–1923.
    [Jewish fairy book]
    Jewish fairy tales / [translated and adapted by] Gerald Friedlander.
        p. cm. — (Dover juvenile classics)
    Originally published: The Jewish fairy book. New York : F.A. Stokes Co., c1920.
    Summary: A collection of Jewish fairy tales assembled from the Talmud and other ancient sources.
    ISBN 0-486-41982-7 (pbk.)
    1. Legends, Jewish. 2. Fairy tales. 3. Jews—Folklore. [1. Jews—Folklore. 2. Folklore. 3. Fairy tales.] I. Title. II. Series.

BM530 .F74 2001
398.2'089'924—dc21

2001042449

Manufactured in the United States of America
Dover Publications, Inc., 31 East 2nd Street, Mineola, N.Y. 11501

Contents

Jewish
Fairy Tales

I. The Magic Apples

ONCE upon a time, a long, long time ago, there lived a happy family in some little town, the name of which I have forgotten. The family consisted of a good Rabbi, his wife and an only daughter. The girl was exceedingly sweet-tempered, and as she grew in years so did she grow in beauty. Every one who saw her fell in love with her at first sight. As is the rule in Jewish homes the girls are never allowed to be out of their parents' sight, and the Rabbi's daughter was no exception to the rule. She was always with her mother or father. The years sped on their course, and one day she was keeping her twentieth birthday. No one till then had had an opportunity of speaking to her, unless her father or mother had been present.

"'Tis time," said the Rabbi to his wife, "to think of our darling daughter's future. She is now twenty years old, and it is not good for a young woman to remain a child. We must let her see just a little of the world, and if the call of love comes to her—why! let her answer; even as you did when I sought your heart and found it."

"Good husband! have you not noticed how very fond our dear daughter is of her cousin Jacob, my sister's only son?"

"Yes, I have seen that they like one another as cousins usually do, but I have also noticed that she seems to prefer her other cousin, David, my brother's only son."

"I cannot say," exclaimed the wife, "that I have noticed this preference. I certainly think that my nephew would make her an excellent husband. Jacob is, as you well know, a most learned man, fit to be a Rabbi, and he is a very good man."

"Yes, yes, dear wife! but I prefer my nephew David as our future son-in-law. He is very clever, and will one day make his mark in the world."

"That is quite likely, dearest husband! but I do not like him as much as I like Jacob."

"But, dearest wife! you know I always preferred David."

"Now listen, best of husbands! I don't want my only daughter to marry David."

"Dear me! sweetest of wives! don't you know that I really do not wish our lovely child to marry her cousin Jacob?"

In this strain they argued till long past midnight, discussing the pros and cons of the two nephews. They could not, however, come to a final decision.

At last they agreed to call together their friends and relatives and to take their advice and to let them settle the question.

Next evening a large party of relatives and friends, including David and Jacob, came together at the Rabbi's house. An excellent repast was provided and in the middle of the meal the Rabbi arose and addressed the company in the following words:—

"My dear wife and I are most happy to see you all at our table. I have brought you together to give us advice. As you know, our dear daughter is now of a marriageable age. The question which perplexes my good wife and me is, whom is she to marry? I have every reason to believe that her cousin David would be an ideal husband. My wife seems to prefer her nephew Jacob. What shall we do? Please help us to decide this very difficult problem. See, here is my daughter at my side, and here are her two cousins. What do you suggest?"

The Rabbi resumed his seat. One of the oldest of the guests arose and said,—

"Good host and hostess! The matter seems to be in my

opinion exceedingly simple, so much so that there was really no occasion to put yourselves to all this trouble in inviting us here to-night. All that you have to do is to put your two nephews before your sweet daughter and to tell her to pick and choose. Let her settle the matter."

The advice appealed to all the company, and the Rabbi asked his daughter to decide between Jacob and David. With a crimson blush on her beautiful face she replied, "I love both my cousins alike, and I cannot show any preference."

"Now," cried the Rabbi, "what are we to do? She cannot marry both."

Again the old guest arose and said:—

"Good host and hostess! It seems after all that you did well in calling us together to help you to find a solution to the problem of your daughter's marriage. What we advise you to do is to give a sum of money, say one hundred pounds, to each of your nephews and to send them out into the wide world to seek their fortunes. Your daughter will wait one year from to-night, and then she will marry the one who returns with the larger fortune."

"Hear! Hear!" cried the guests, and the nephews also appeared to be satisfied.

The Rabbi expressed his entire approval. All present agreed that this was a fair and proper solution.

The party broke up and all went home satisfied with the result at which they had so unanimously arrived.

That same night the Rabbi in the presence of his wife and daughter gave the two nephews one hundred pounds apiece and blessed them, wishing each one good luck. Next morning the two nephews set out on their quest of gaining a fortune. They traveled all the morning together and at noon they came to a market town. They resolved to buy something with their money and on the morrow they would part and each one try his luck. David invested his money in a large stock of silk. "I will," said he to himself, "be able to sell this at a good profit and I will buy a further supply, and by the time the year is round I shall have put by a good sum." Jacob bought a number of jewels which he put in his pocket. They had agreed to spend the night together at the inn in the market town. David had his bales of silk brought into the inn and carried into their bedroom. After they had enjoyed a good supper they retired to their room, both very tired after their day's tramp.

Unknown to themselves they had been watched by a gang of thieves, who broke into the inn in the middle of the night. They found their way to the bedroom where the cousins were fast asleep. The thieves emptied the pockets of both men, and glad in having secured the precious jewels they hastened away. They did not remove the bales of silk, for this might have attracted attention in the streets. With the break of dawn the two cousins arose and said their morning prayers, asking Heaven to prosper them on their way. Whilst David was arranging with the host for the removal of the bales of silk, Jacob cried aloud,—

"Cousin David! I have been robbed. I showed you the jewels last night just before we went to bed, and you saw me replace them in my pocket. Now my pocket is empty. Do not think I grieve because I have been robbed, but I am overwhelmed with sorrow, for I fear I have now lost the hand of our beautiful cousin whom I love with all my heart. What shall I do?"

"Now, good cousin, do not lose heart. You have a whole year in which you can make a fortune. Of course I now have a great advantage over you, but that is not my fault. Should I return home I will tell our uncle and aunt that you have gone on a long journey, but that you will return within the twelve months. Now go in God's name, and may good luck attend you."

Thus they parted and each went his own way. David was happy and confident, whilst his cousin was sad and despondent. He said to himself: "Uncle is always right in saying that cousin David is very clever. I also believe that he will become a rich and great man. Dear me! What a fool I was to put all my money in a handful of jewels. Alas!

before twelve hours have passed I am penniless. I was never born to be a merchant. I am a student and I ought not to meddle with things which I do not understand. David will, I suppose, marry my lovely cousin, and I shall be unhappy all my life."

David prospered and at the end of six months he returned home. He went to visit his aunt and uncle. They inquired after Jacob and were satisfied to learn that he had gone on a long journey. The Rabbi's daughter asked David when did he think Jacob would return. David replied that he did not expect to see him for another six months.

Meanwhile Jacob knew that the only hope for his future peace of mind lay in his pursuit of knowledge. He realized that he was hardly likely to become a rich man. He therefore determined to spend his year of probation in study. "This," said he to himself, "will be my comfort and I may be of use to my fellow beings."

On and on he trudged till he arrived at last at the Jewish College at Sura in Babylon. He entered the College hall and sat by himself in a dark corner, for he was ashamed to show himself before the teachers and pupils owing to his shabby appearance. His boots were worn out and his clothes were threadbare. He listened to the lecture given by the head of the College and followed every point with the deepest interest. The pupils were asked to solve a difficult problem arising out of the lecture, and to be prepared with their solution on the following day.

At sundown all the pupils left the College and poor Jacob remained behind. He had nowhere to go for the night's shelter. He thought he would spend the evening in reading the Talmud so as to be able to solve the problem set by the lecturer. He was so very tired and hungry that it was not long before he fell fast asleep over the book in front of him. It was a sleep of sheer exhaustion. His eyes were barely shut by the bands of sleep when he began to dream. He saw the beautiful girl in his uncle's house and she looked more lovely than he had ever seen her. This vision faded away and he saw a very old man with a snow white long beard and such a noble face. He heard the old man's voice, it was like an angel's song, so winning and so gentle. The voice said, "I am Elijah, the prophet. I come to give thee the greatest treasure on earth, knowledge and understanding. Make good use of it and thou wilt be blessed. Farewell." The vision faded and Jacob awoke. He felt refreshed and happy, for he had seen his beloved and the great prophet Elijah. Elijah, like the good fairy, is always at hand to comfort the sorrowful, to cheer the despondent and to help those in distress.

Jacob now thought of the problem set to the pupils. The solution flashed through his mind; he saw the whole problem in all its bearings. He wrote out the answer on the table in front of the teacher's seat. When the class assembled next morning the teacher asked whether there was any one who could answer the question set the previous day. No one replied. His eyes fell and he read with no little surprise the correct solution written on the table. Turning to his pupils he asked, "Who has written this answer?" There was again no reply. The answer was perfectly correct and he added: "I feel very proud to know that one of the class has been so very diligent. I rejoice to think that this pupil is so modest, for he is not anxious to disclose his identity. The true scholar is always humble."

Again that day he set a new question, more difficult than the one set on the previous day. Again the same result ensued. The correct answer was written on the table opposite to the teacher's place. He again asked, "Who has written this answer?" The pupils were silent. For a third time a fresh problem was set. The teacher was determined to find out the intelligent and modest pupil whose answers had been so accurate. He bored a small hole in the wall and watched events from the next room. When all the students had left the class-room he saw a stranger leave the corner and advance to the table. He was dressed in threadbare garments and looked very famished. He saw him write out the answer and then return to the corner, where he fell asleep. The teacher had seen enough. He now knew why his own pupils had not been able to admit that one of them had written the answers to his questions.

Next morning he repeated his usual question, "Who has written this answer on my table?" Once more there was silence. He now requested the stranger to come forward. The latter immediately did as he was bidden.

"Did you write this answer to my question?"

"I did, honored Rabbi!"

"Why did you come here?"

"To learn, good master! I wish to stay here three months and then to return to my home."

"You are most welcome, but not as a disciple."

"Why not, may I ask?"

"You are wise enough to teach these my pupils. If you care to stay with us we shall be not only thankful but also honored. As long as you remain you will please do me the favor of being my guest."

"These kind words, great master! touch my heart, but I have really journeyed here in order to sit at your feet and learn. I left home nearly four months ago and I must be back within one year. Pray accede to my wish and accept me as a pupil."

"Your extreme modesty is very becoming. You are a master in Israel, and there is nothing that I can teach you. I shall yet find that you are able to teach me. To-morrow you will begin your duties as a new teacher in our college."

That day the Rabbi took Jacob home with him to live.

Next day Jacob began to teach. The disciples were greatly surprised at his vast knowledge and admired his marked ability as a teacher. He was soon beloved by all who knew him. At the end of three months he told his good friend, the Rabbi, that, much to his regret, he would have to take his leave and return home.

"Stay with me and you shall wed my daughter, who loves you!" the Rabbi said.

"I greatly appreciate your extreme kindness and I am

glad to think I have found favor in the eyes of your good daughter, but my heart is entwined with the heart of my cousin. I have pledged my word to see her in less than five months." He then told the kind-hearted Rabbi of the circumstance that led to his being there. He told him how his cousin David and he had received £100 each and that the one who should have at the end of twelve months the larger fortune would receive the hand of the beautiful daughter of their uncle. "I have determined to be home in time for the wedding, even though it may not be my good fortune to be the lucky husband," he added.

"Go in peace," said the Rabbi, "and God prosper your way."

Jacob started on his return journey in a happy mood. He was returning with a treasure far more precious than the jewels which had been stolen from him. Elijah's blessing was indeed something worth having. On and on did he tramp for the best part of the day, for he stopped neither to eat nor to rest, so fiercely did the desire to see the face of his beloved burn within him. At last his feet refused to carry him any further. He was also very faint; hunger and thirst began to claim attention, and he did not know how to satisfy them. He looked about and saw on his left a fine tree with very large apples, as bright as silver. He dragged himself to the tree and picked off an apple. He then seated himself under the tree and began to eat the fruit. The taste was very bitter and he had barely eaten half when he noticed a strange feeling coming over him. He felt sick, and his skin seemed to grow cold. His hands were as white as snow, like a leper's skin. He looked at his feet and legs and they were also white. He knew that it was leprosy.

"I have eaten," said he, "poisonous fruit. Woe is me! Surely this is not Elijah's blessing. I will rest here no longer; I will go on my way till I fall to the ground. To die would be a release." On he went, and after a few steps he came to another tall tree laden with very large apples with a golden hue. "I will taste," said he, "one of these apples, they look so lovely. If I die well and good, for what am I to do now that I am a leper?"

He plucked an apple and began to eat it. It had a most delicious taste, as sweet as honey, as juicy as a grape. He felt ever so much better, his faintness disappeared and, miracle of miracles! the awful white color of his hands vanished. His leprosy was cured. He thanked God for His wonderful mercy and love.

He felt himself renewed with vigor and life. "This is all indeed a blessing," he mused. "I must go back and fetch some of the silver apples," and he did so. He then picked off a few of the golden apples and continued his journey. At last he came to the capital of the kingdom where he had been born. His own home, where his lovely cousin also lived, was situated in a small town not very far from the capital. As soon as he entered the city he heard the sound of lamentation. All joy and happiness had fled; sorrow and weeping met his gaze. He feared that some dread disaster had befallen the city. He inquired of the first person whom he met concerning the misfortune.

"What's the meaning of all this sorrow?" he asked.

"Why, our dear old King," came the reply, "has a most terrible attack of leprosy. From the sole of his foot to the crown of his head, his skin is leprous. Poor King, he will not live long, for all his doctors are unable to cure him."

Jacob listened with rapt attention and passed on. He now betook himself to the King's palace. When he came there he knocked at the door. He stood waiting for some one to come out and ask him what he wanted. At last the palace door was opened and the royal butler asked Jacob why he had knocked.

"I must see His Majesty at once."

"What is your business?"

"I will cure His Majesty."

"What and who are you?"

"I am Jacob the Jew, a Rabbi and a doctor."

The butler then brought him to his royal master. Jacob saw that the King's head and face were covered, for he did not like his servants to gaze upon him in his terrible condition.

"What is your wish?" cried the King. "Have you also come to torment me by promising to heal me, knowing all the while that you are deceiving me?"

"Nay, your Majesty; God has given me wisdom and understanding. I am sure I can help your Majesty to be restored to good health."

"If it be as you say, I will give you half my kingdom, and fifty thousand pounds. Should you fail, mark you, you will lose your head."

"I agree," cried Jacob, making an obeisance.

"One condition do I make," said the King, "and that is— you must not have recourse to any species of magical art or sorcery. I will not allow you to use any charms or spells."

"Your Majesty has already heard that I am a Jew. Our holy religion has always forbidden us to practice sorcery."

"Quite so, but how do you propose to cure me?"

"Your Majesty must first of all leave yourself in God's hands. I do not boast of any special skill, but God has given us mortals certain knowledge and insight. I will do my best, and if you trust in the Heavenly Father, I think you will be quite satisfied."

The King was greatly pleased by these modest remarks, and he told Jacob that he was satisfied with him.

"But," he said, "I should just like to know the nature of your treatment."

"At first your gracious Majesty will become worse, you will feel sick, weak and very depressed. This is the first stage, for leprosy must be very acute before it can be radically cured."

"Stay," cried the King, "if I become worse I shall die."

"Not so, your Majesty! You will die if you do not become worse; for there is no cure for your disease in its present form. I will cure your Majesty if you will submit to my treatment."

"I agree," the King said, "and now proceed with your cure."

Jacob asked for a supply of sugar, two knives, and two plates. When these things were brought to him, he took from his pocket one of the silver apples and cut it up into small pieces. He put sugar over these pieces and gave the plate to the King, saying,—

"Your Majesty will be good enough to eat this sour apple, every piece. I have added sugar to make the taste more palatable. You will feel very uncomfortable for a while, but as I have already said, this is absolutely necessary."

The King obeyed Jacob's order and ate the pieces of the apple. No sooner had he done this, than he began to moan. "I am much worse, I am dying," he murmured.

"Not so, your Majesty! The cure is already beginning to act."

"Look at my hand," exclaimed the King, "it is now as white as the driven snow; it is so cold, it is lifeless."

"Patience, your Majesty! In one hour you will take another apple and your leprosy will vanish. I will stake my life on your Majesty's complete recovery."

Meanwhile he began to cut into small pieces one of the golden apples. There was no need to put sugar on this fruit. When, at last, he gave it to the King there was no more grumbling. The King ate it with relish and said he was sorry there was no more left.

"I never tasted such wonderful fruit in all my life," he cried in a happy voice. "I feel quite well again now. See my skin—it is no longer leprous. You are a great doctor and you have saved my life. I am so much better, I shall be able to get out of my bed. I am indeed grateful and I will keep my promise; fifty thousand pounds shall be paid to you this day and you now own half of my kingdom."

"Your gracious Majesty!" cried Jacob. "May God preserve your life and give you length of days. I do not desire to accept all you offer. I ask for a small gift, and that is— give me the right of owning the small town, not very far from your capital, where my uncle and aunt live, where my home is."

"Most gladly will I do this."

The King caused letters-patent to be issued declaring Jacob to be the Prince of that town. He also gave him a valuable gold chain as a mark of his royal favor.

"Now, Sire! pray let me go," said Jacob, "and take possession of my town."

"Go, and twenty knights of my retinue shall accompany you."

Away they went, a fine procession to behold. News spread far and wide that the new Prince of the town was about to enter his new territory. The inhabitants came forth to greet him. When he came to his castle he was met by a deputation consisting of the most respected of the citizens. Jacob was dressed in splendid attire with the golden chain about his neck. He had changed considerably since he had left home and he was not recognized. Among the members of the deputation was Jacob's uncle, the Rabbi.

Jacob began to speak: "I am right glad to see you all here in my castle. As the Prince of this town I will henceforth take up my abode within these walls. Your lives and mine must be identified. Your joys shall be mine and I will share your sorrows. You will be happy to learn that our gracious King is now restored to health. It was my good fortune to help His Majesty to regain his health and he in his kindness of heart has made me Prince and owner of this town. I shall respect all my friends, be their religion what it may, for the good of all nations and religions are sure to inherit eternal bliss. Please let me know when you are about to celebrate any family festivity, and I will be present."

"Now that is very fortunate," exclaimed Jacob's uncle. "In three days I shall have my only daughter married, and your presence will increase our happiness."

"I hope so," said Jacob with a happy smile, "and now farewell till we meet at the wedding."

The deputation withdrew, well satisfied with the courtesy shown to them by their new ruler.

Three days later Jacob betook himself to his uncle's house, just as the wedding ceremony was about to commence. He was received with marked attention by his uncle and aunt, who had not the faintest idea that the new ruler was their nephew. Turning to the Rabbi, Jacob said,—

"May I be introduced to the bride before the ceremony takes place?"

"Of course you can," exclaimed the happy father.

No sooner did his daughter look at Jacob than she cried aloud,—

"Father! Mother! this is my cousin."

"True," exclaimed Jacob. "Listen, good friends. To-day is the anniversary of our last gathering here, when you, dear uncle, gave me one hundred pounds and you also gave my cousin David, whom I see here, a similar sum. I do not know whether David has turned his hundred pounds into a very large fortune. I, for my part, am the owner of this town and that means a fairly large fortune. Our sweet and lovely cousin has agreed to marry the one who has the larger fortune. His Majesty the King has even been good enough to promise to give me half of his kingdom as well as fifty thousand pounds. Need I say more?"

The remarks were greeted with applause by all present, and David agreed that the bride had been fairly won by Jacob. Every one was thoroughly delighted except David, who slipped away and was heard of no more.

Jacob and his wife lived a very happy life, blessed with worldly prosperity. Elijah's blessing was realized to the full, and Jacob never forgot his wonderful dream in the College at Sura in Babylon.

Maàseh Book (*Chap Book*),
ed. Rödelheim 72d–74b.

II. The Wise Merchant

THERE once lived a merchant who had an only son. Wherever the father went his son accompanied him, for the former was somewhat advanced in years and the son did not like his father to travel alone. In those days traveling was not a pleasure. It made no difference whether one went by land or sea, robbers were rarely absent. The father and son dealt in precious jewels, and it once happened that they set out on a sea voyage. They carried with them a large box full of valuable gems.

Father and son occupied one cabin and they had the large box placed there for safety. One of the crew had discovered that the merchant had very valuable treasures in his cabin. He told this to the rest of the crew, who were a gang of thieves. It happened by chance that when the crew were discussing this matter, the old merchant overheard part of their conversation. This is what he heard,—

"Now we have a splendid opportunity of becoming very wealthy."

"How so?" cried the rest.

"Why, I was this morning in the cabin of the merchant and his son to find out what they have in their box. I found the key in the lock and I opened the box. It is full of pearls and diamonds."

"What do you propose?" they asked him. "Speak, for you are our leader."

"My plan," he answered, "is very simple. Tomorrow when we are on the high seas, far away from the coast, one of us will start a conversation with the merchant and lead him to the side of the ship. I will keep watch, and when he is looking out to sea, I will run across the deck and fall against him and throw him into the water. When the son learns of his father's death he will be overwhelmed with grief. It will then be very easy for one of us to enter the cabin and to remove the jewels from the box, leaving the latter in its place in the cabin."

"How about the spoil?" they asked.

"Naturally we will divide," said he, "all we obtain quite fairly. There are seven of us and we will each have an equal share. This will be enough. We shall all be rich, and we can give up our wretched life on the water and start afresh when we reach port."

"We agree," they cried unanimously.

The merchant had not lost a single word of this very interesting proposal. He smiled and said to himself,—

"Well does the proverb say: 'Man proposes, but God disposes.' How am I to outwit these thieves?"

He walked up and down the deck, thinking as hard as he could. He then looked for his son, whom he found in the cabin. They had made a mutual agreement that one of them should spend the best part of the day in the cabin, to keep an eye on their treasure.

"My son," said he, "by God's mercy I have discovered a villainous plot. The crew on board are a gang of thieves and murderers. I have overheard part of their plan. I firmly believe that I did so by God's will, for the Almighty watches over all of us and sends us warning when danger threatens us. My life is in danger and our fortune likewise. Let us act with great caution. If you promise to do exactly as I tell you, I think all will be well."

"I promise, dear father; what am I to do?"

"We must pretend to quarrel. You are to begin by being very insolent to me. I, of course, will rebuke you. Pay no heed to my rebuke, but abuse me and insult me. I will again rebuke you and then I will strike you, calling you 'a rebellious son worthy of death.' Pay no heed, but raise your hand as though you intended to strike me. Our quarrel will attract the attention of the crew, and when they are eye-witnesses I will rush away to the cabin and bring forth the large box which contains our fortune. I will turn to the crew and cry aloud: 'See how I now punish my rebellious son. This box is full of jewels, it is all our fortune. I had rather be a beggar than allow such a wicked son to go unpunished. Into the sea I cast our wealth, which I earned with the sweat of my brow.' I shall then throw the box into the sea, and whilst I am about to do this I will open the lid and let them see the jewels, as otherwise they will imagine that I am bluffing them."

"Will you really throw all the jewels into the sea, dear father?"

"Of course I will, dear boy."

"But we shall be poor."

"Better poor and alive than rich and dead. Do you agree, my boy?"

"Yes, I will do exactly as you have told me."

They immediately began to play their part, for they realized that the sooner the jewels were overboard the safer it would be. They went on deck and began to talk in an excited manner. High words began to pass between them. The crew listened. At last they began to abuse one another and the quarrel seemed so serious that all the crew assembled to look on and enjoy the fun. When the father struck the son, they seemed to the crew to be two madmen. But they could hardly believe their eyes when they saw the old man dragging the precious jewel box across the deck.

"What's he going to do now?" they asked one another in bated breath. "Perhaps he will scatter the gems over the deck and we shall have a lovely scramble."

They watched with strained eyes every movement of the merchant.

"Look, look!" they shouted, "the madman is throwing the whole box, worth millions, overboard."

The rest of the voyage was spent in peace and safety.

There was now no reason to kill the merchant. When they came to port, the merchant and his son hastened to the magistrates and laid a charge of attempted murder and robbery against the entire crew. The police came on board and arrested the rogues. When the case came before the magistrates, the merchant said he would be satisfied with the repayment of the value of the jewels which he had so wisely sacrificed in order to save his life. The magistrates agreed to this proposal, and ordered the crew to refund the sum demanded. They found ways and means to do this, so that the merchant had not only saved his life but, at the same time, he had managed to save his fortune.

Eccles. Rabbah, Eccles. iii. 6.

III. Heavenly Treasures

IN the first century of the common era there was a King named Monobazus. He ruled over the land of Adiabene near Assyria. By birth a heathen, he ultimately embraced the Jewish religion. His example was followed by his wife Queen Helena, and their son Izates, who in time succeeded his father on the throne.

Now it happened, shortly after Monobazus became a Jew, that his subjects were sorely oppressed by a very severe famine. Many of the people died of starvation and want. When King Monobazus saw the plight of his people he opened the royal treasuries and distributed all his wealth among the unfortunate poor. His noble conduct displeased his rich relatives, who came to him in order to reproach him. They asked him: "Is it true that thou art thinking of opening the royal treasury of thy late father, our wise and beloved King?"

Monobazus: "It is quite true; in fact I have already opened all the royal treasuries."

Then they asked him: "May we inquire what purpose hast thou in view?"

Monobazus: "My purpose is to feed the starving poor in my kingdom."

This answer led them to say: "Thy fathers gathered treasures, but thou hast squandered them."

Monobazus: "My fathers laid up treasures upon earth, but I lay up treasures in Heaven. My fathers gathered them into treasuries over which the hand of man hath

18

power; I have stored mine in a treasury over which the hand of man hath no power. My fathers gathered that which bears no fruit, whilst I have gathered that which yields fruit. My fathers gathered wealth: whilst I have gathered souls. My fathers gathered for this world; I have gathered for the world to come, even as it is said in Holy Writ.—'Treasures of wickedness profit nothing: but charity delivereth from death'" (Prov. x. 2).

Palestinian Talmud, Peah i, 1, 15b.

IV. King Solomon's Carpet

WHEN the Holy One, blessed be He, bestowed the kingdom of David upon Solomon his son, He also gave him power to rule over the beasts of the field, the birds of the air, the fish of the sea, the spirits and all things in Creation. On the day of his coronation the demons brought to his palace a magic carpet. Ashmodai their chief, in presenting it to Solomon, exclaimed,—

"Great King, O son of David! our master and ruler! Know thou that this green silken carpet, so beautifully embroidered, will carry thee whithersoever thou wilt go. It is thine as a gift from thy ruler and master, the King of Kings. Its length is sixty miles and its breadth is as long as its length."

Ashmodai and the demons vanished, and Solomon stood gazing at the wonderful gift.

Now King Solomon had four chieftains ever at his command. There was Asaph son of Berechjah, who ruled over the children of men. Then Ramerat was the chief of the genii. The king of the beasts was the lion. The eagle ruled over the birds. When Solomon traveled the wind was ever with him waiting to obey the royal behest. When it pleased him he would take his morning meal in the east and, on that same day, he would sup in the west of the world.

There was also Ashmodai, King of the demons. Solomon could summon him to his presence by rubbing the magic ring which he wore on his right hand. This ring was engraved with the Holy Name of God. Solomon sent some of the demons to India whence they brought him wonderful water to irrigate his plants, which never withered. These plants supplied him with wonderful leaves with which he cured disease and sickness. In summer and winter lovely roses adorned his table. He loved to try and understand all things. In order to learn the different ways of men he disguised himself and mixed with all sorts and conditions of people. He was a man who had strung many experiences upon the chain of his remarkable life. Tales could be told of the varied phases of his career. Sometimes he was rich, at other times he was poor. He was King and again a beggar. Now let us listen to a brief account of one day's story in the extraordinary life of this wonderful monarch.

One fine summer's day he arose early in the morning. He was staying in his beautiful palace in Jerusalem. He betook himself as soon as he had dressed to the Holy Temple for the morning service of praise. He listened with bowed head to the sweet song of the Levites. They were singing the beautiful psalms written by his beloved father David. He loved to hear the sweet strains of the Temple organ. He joined in the responses with the rest of the worshipers. After the termination of Divine Service he returned to his palace. He then transacted the various affairs of state. The rest of the day was free. He resolved to spend it on his magic carpet. He would travel abroad and see something of the world.

He took the wonderful carpet out of his pocket. How it glittered in the sunshine! When it was spread out it looked like a sea of gold. He delighted to look at its wonderful embroidery, depicting all the marvels of the universe. He beheld pictures in silk, gold and jewels—there were mountains, trees, birds and beasts, giants and demons. When he stepped upon the carpet he ordered his servants to place his wonderful throne on it. When he sat thereon he sometimes imagined that he was the absolute ruler in heaven above, on the earth beneath, and in the waters

under the earth. His pride and vanity grew at the expense
of his faith in God. At such moments his humility forsook
him. He almost thought that he was a god.

No sooner was he on his magic carpet than he commanded one hundred thousand troops to be his escort.
He touched his magic ring and said,—

"I will now set out for Damascus, where I will take my
breakfast."

In the twinkling of an eye Damascus lay at his feet. The
wind, bearing up the carpet, awaited further orders and
the carpet was stationary betwixt heaven and earth. The
genii served the breakfast which Solomon ate with relish,
for it was now the fourth hour of the day and he had
tasted nothing since his supper on the previous evening.

"Perhaps," said he to himself, "I will sup tonight in
Media. Meanwhile, I will traverse the world, my domains,
and see how life looks in the different lands. Verily I am
great and mighty. There has never been any monarch in
all time who has become as famous as I am. The Holy One,
blessed be He, has given me unbounded wisdom, understanding, knowledge and intelligence. I am Solomon the
Wise and I rule beasts, tame and wild, birds and fish, the
spirits and demons, aye, all things in creation. I am truly a
wonderful King."

At that moment the wind changed its course and the
carpet tilted somewhat, so that forty thousand soldiers
fell off the carpet.

They fell down and down till they reached the earth.
This annoyed Solomon immensely and he began to rebuke the wind. He cried to it in a sharp voice,—

"Wind, return to thy former position, dost thou hear?"

"I hear very well, mighty son of David! and I will do as
thou dost bid me, provided thou dost also return to the
humble faith in God which David thy father taught thee.
Did he not say: 'The meek shall inherit the earth?'[1] God
loves humility."

---

1. Ps. xxxvii. 11.

In that moment Solomon was abashed. The rebuke of the wind had been fully deserved by the pride and vanity of the King. The wind bore up the carpet which now resumed its level position. Again the King rubbed his magic ring and commanded the wind to move on. The carpet flew through space and was just passing over a deep valley when Solomon cried, "Halt!" Below there were tens of thousands of tiny black ants. Solomon was somewhat taken aback to hear the voice of one ant crying to its little fellows: "Take cover! lest ye be crushed by the mighty army of the great King Solomon, the Servant of God."

Solomon commanded the wind to let the carpet fall nearer to the valley. He then cried aloud in a terrible fury: "We will descend to earth."

He commanded Ashmodai to appear before him. When the King of the demons saw Solomon on his wonderful throne he made obeisance and said,—

"Command, great Master, and thy wishes shall be fulfilled."

"Go, Ashmodai, and bring before me the ants in yonder valley."

The ants swarmed on the earth over which the magic carpet was hanging. Solomon said,—

"Where is the little ant that gave the command to all the other ants saying: 'Take cover' lest ye be crushed by my army?"

The little black ant came a few inches forward and said,—

"I am the one that gave this command."

"Who art thou?"

"I am the queen of the ants."

"What is thy name?"

"Machashamah."

"Now tell me, little queen, why didst thou give thy command to the other ants?"

"I was afraid that the ants might venture to gaze at thy magic carpet and thereby they would interrupt our service of praise with which we glorify God all day long. If we cease to praise our Creator we deserve to die, for then we are of no use in the world."

"Is it not true that ants also work?"

"It is true, but our work is also prayer. Idleness leads to pride and vanity, whereas toil makes one humble and meek. Dost thou not think likewise, O wise King?"

"Never mind what I think, but let me rather ask thee a simple question."

"Dost thou not know, King Solomon, that it is not seemly for the one who asks a question to be on high, whilst the one who has to reply is down below?"

"What dost thou wish me to do, Machashamah?"

"Why, lift me up, of course, O wisest of Kings."

King Solomon bent down and lifted up the ant. He placed the tiny insect on his magic carpet just in front of his golden throne. He turned to it and sat on his throne exclaiming,—

"Is it all right now?"

"No, it is not all right, great King."

"Why not, Machashamah?"

"It is also unbecoming for the questioner to be seated whilst the one who gives the answer is standing on a lower level. Take me upon thine hand and I will answer thy question—if I am able."

Solomon obeyed the ant.

"Is there any one in all the world greater than I am?"

"To be sure there is."

"Who is it, Machashamah?"

"It is I."

"How dost thou dare to say this?"

"Because it is the truth."

"Prove it."

"If I were not greater than thou art, surely the Holy One, blessed be He, would not have sent thee to me to take me upon thine hand."

When Solomon heard these words he was beside himself with fury. He cast the ant off his hand to the carpet and said to it,—

"Ant! thou knowest not to whom thou art speaking. Thou dost not really know who and what I am. I am Solomon, son of David, of blessed memory; I rule all things on earth, in the air and in the sea. I have a magic ring and a magic carpet, and what hast thou?"

"O Solomon! thou wilt one day be the food for the ants; they will feast on thy body in the grave, therefore boast not."

At that same moment Solomon fell upon his face and was put to shame by the truth spoken by the little queen of the ants.

He then commanded Ashmodai to remove all the ants to their former haunts, and calling to the wind to carry his carpet on high he said: "Away!"

The wind began to lift up the magic carpet, and as it was about to fly away into space, Machashamah cried out,—

"Farewell, King Solomon, forget not to praise God and to labor for the glory of His Holy Name. Remember all I have told thee and boast no more."

Solomon continued his journey betwixt heaven and earth. On and on he went, over hill and dale, across rivers and mountains. At last he came to a vast desert and noticed a huge mound. Coming nearer he saw that it was a large building almost entirely covered by the sand of the desert. He called to the wind to slacken its speed, saying that he wished to descend to the earth. His magic carpet glided down to the earth and Solomon stepped upon the sand. He at once summoned Ashmodai and bade him fold up the carpet. When this was done he put it into his pocket. He then asked his Princes and servants if they knew what sort of building it was. They shook their heads and told him they had never been in that desert before.

"See!" cried he, "it is much larger than my palace in the Lebanon. I will enter and see what sort of place it is. Find the entrance."

His Princes and servants looked on all sides for a door, but their efforts were all in vain.

In his despair he again summoned Ashmodai.

"What is thy wish, O master?"

"I am vexed because my Princes and servants cannot find an entrance to this building. What can you suggest?"

"Sovereign master! I will order my demons to ascend to the roof, and perhaps they may be able to find there a man or an animal. Dost thou approve?"

"Be it so, and let there be no delay."

Ashmodai bowed to the ground and vanished. The King of the demons bade some of his servants among the genii and demons to ascend to the roof and to report to him what was to be seen. They ascended, and having looked around they descended. They returned to Ashmodai and said,—

"Royal master! We saw not a son of man upon the roof, but we found a large mountain eagle sitting in her nest."

Ashmodai reported the result to Solomon, who commanded him to bring to his presence the sea eagle, the prince of the birds. When the sea eagle came before Solomon, he ordered it to fetch the mountain eagle from the roof of the building. This was done. As soon as the mountain eagle saw Solomon, she began to utter the praise of God and then she greeted the King.

The King looked at the old bird and said,—

"What is thy name?"

"Alanad."

"How old art thou?"

"My years number seven hundred."

"Hast thou ever seen the door of the building on the roof of which thou hast thy nest?"

"O King! mayest thou live forever! By the life of thy head I know nothing of the door. I have a brother two hundred years older than I am. He is more learned than I, perhaps he can tell thee, O King, what thou desirest to know. He lives in a nest a little above my home."

Solomon again commanded the sea eagle to fetch Alanad's brother. When he came before the King he was praising the great and good Creator of all things. He then greeted Solomon, who asked him,—

"What is thy name?"

"Alôf."

"What is thy age?"

"The days of my life are nine hundred years."

"Dost thou know where the entrance to yonder building is situated?"

"Mighty King! By thy life I assure thee that I know not where the entrance is. May be that my brother, who is four hundred years older than I am, can tell thee. His nest is a little beyond mine."

Once more Solomon told the sea eagle to bring this old bird before him. "Do not forget," he added, "to carry it if it cannot fly." It was brought before the King, and like its brother and sister it was praising God.

After their mutual greeting Solomon inquired,—

"How old art thou?"

"I am one thousand and three hundred years old."

"What is thy name?"

"My father called me Alta-'amar."

"Hast thou seen any entrance to this building here?"

"By thy head, O wise King! I know it not, but well do I remember my late father speaking of its golden door. This was situated on the side looking towards sunset. Owing to the time that has passed since it was last opened, when it admitted a mighty King, it has been covered over by the sand of the desert. For this reason it is now hidden from view. If it please thee, O wise Solomon, let thy command go forth that the sand shall disappear. Forgive my presumption in giving advice to one so wise."

"I thank thee, Alta-'amar, for thy advice, but I do not see how I can cause the sand to vanish. Can you suggest how it might be done?"

"Command the wind to blow the sand away on the side facing sunset and the entrance will be seen."

"Many thanks, and now farewell."

The three old eagles returned to their nests. Solomon commanded the wind to blow with all its might and to drive away the sand on the west side of the building. In a few minutes a wonderful sight met the King's gaze. Lo! there stood a beautiful portico, and Solomon entered. He came to a massive iron door. Time had made her inroads and the iron was very rusty. There was an inscription in Hebrew which Solomon began to read. The following was what he read,—

"O children of men! be it known to you that I and my Princes dwelt in this magic palace for very many years in joy and contentment. At last hunger invaded its walls and entered within. We ground our best pearls with the little corn we could obtain, but all in vain. Hunger drove us forth and we left our home for the eagles to take our place. At length we grew weary of life, for we were faint in our souls and bodies and we laid ourselves down to sleep in the dust. We told the eagles to say to all comers, who might ask them about this wonderful palace, 'We found it already built. Let no man enter unless he be a King or a prophet. If he desire to enter let him dig up the sand on the right side of the portico, where he will see a crystal box. He must break this box open in order to get the keys of the palace.'"

Solomon told his Princes and attendants that he would inspect the palace by himself. He followed the directions which he had read and he was very happy when he found the crystal box. When he had broken it open he took out the keys. Without any delay he opened the iron door and entered the palace.

He was greatly surprised to see that another door now faced him. It was of burnished gold. He found the key to open this door, and when he had opened it he was amazed to find another door in front of him. After he had opened it, he entered a large room full of pearls and pre-cious jewels. In the next room he found gold and silver coins in large boxes. He went on and saw a large court-yard. Its pavement was of gold. He passed on and entered a magnificent dining hall, very spacious and lofty. It was perfumed with the scent of paradise. "Never have I seen such a noble room. It is truly fit for a King," exclaimed

Solomon in astonishment and delight. The dining hall had another courtyard at its further end. Solomon passed through and saw in the center the image of a scorpion cast in silver. He removed it and found beneath it a large ring set in a wooden trap-door. He lifted up the latter and saw a secret staircase. He descended and found treasures uncounted, precious jewels and money. He went on and came to a door of silver on which he read these words,—

"The lord of this magic palace was a King, mighty and honored. At his presence lions trembled and bears fainted, for he was a mighty warrior. Here he lived in bliss and peace, ruling the lands east and west. After many happy years his time to die came, alas! all too soon, and when he died his crown fell off his head. If thou art stout-hearted enough to enter the next room, thou wilt see wonderful and terrible sights. If thou art faint-hearted return and begone."

Solomon knew no fear; did he not wear on the little finger of his right hand his magic ring? He went to the next room and opened the door. He entered and found a sack tied at its mouth. He untied it and found that it contained rubies, emeralds and diamonds. He saw a large label attached to the sack and he read the following words written thereon,—

"The owners of these gems were very wealthy men; their treasures are here, but they are dead. Worldly treasures remain on earth when their owners pass from this life. Reader! Ask thyself these questions and find their answers. How long shall I stand on earth? What will happen to me? How much will I eat and drink? How often shall I dress myself in beautiful garments? How often shall I make others afraid and how often shall I feel afraid? Son of man! be not deceived by time. Thou also wilt wither and pass away, leaving this magic palace, and thou wilt sleep beneath the soft earth. Do not be in too great a hurry, thou hast little that is really thine, for the world takes from one to give to another. Take provision with thee on thy last journey. Prepare whilst it is still day what thou mayest require when it grows dark. Thou also wilt pass from the light into the darkness where is the shadow of death. Thou knowest not the day of thy last journey."

Solomon read and re-read the strange words. When he came to the end of the room he was somewhat startled to see in front of him a life-size image of a man seated on a throne with a crown upon his head and a scepter in his hand. Solomon gazed at it for a few seconds—it seemed to be alive. Did the lips tremble? Did not the eyes open? Did not the scepter seem to move? Solomon advanced nearer and nearer, and at last he put his hand upon the scepter and tried to remove it. He could not, the hand held it fast. He now put his hand on the crown, when he was terrified to see the lips open and he heard the image cry in a terrible voice that shook the palace,—

"Come hither, ye children of Satan! See, Solomon, King of Israel, is here. He has come across the desert to destroy you in this your magic palace."

Whilst the image was speaking fire and smoke came forth through its nostrils. At that second horrible screaming and wild tumult, as loud as the crash of thunder, deafened Solomon's ears. The very earth seemed to quake. Solomon knew that now was the moment for him to be mastered or to overcome his foes. He cried in a bold voice,—

"Hearken to my words, ye children of Satan! You think you can frighten me? You are mightily mistaken. I am Solomon, son of David, I come here in the name of the Holy One to rule and subdue all things which He has created. If you presume to rebel against me I will punish you with terrible chastisement. Now begone, and let there be peace wherever the children of men dwell."

He then pronounced the Name of God and all was as silent as when he entered the room. Then the image fell to the ground and the children of Satan vanished. They hastened on and on till they came to the great sea, into which they threw themselves.

Solomon again advanced to the fallen image and took a

silver plate out of its mouth. It had a strange inscription which he was unable to read. He returned to his retinue and handed round the silver plate, asking them to read it. They could not do so. He then told them what he had seen and done in the magic palace.

"You know," he exclaimed, "how very much I have exerted myself to explore this wonderful palace, and now that I have seen all it contains and I have learnt its secrets, I am puzzled by this little inscription. I must find out what it means."

He rubbed his magic ring and summoned Ashmodai.

"Good Ashmodai, find some one who can read the writing on this plate."

Ashmodai made an obeisance and vanished. In a moment he returned with a child of the desert. The lad was dressed like a shepherd boy. As soon as he saw Solomon he fell on his face to the ground. The King told him to rise. He obeyed and said to the King,—

"Tell me what is troubling thee, O mighty Solomon, wisest of mortals!"

"Take this silver tablet and read its inscription."

The child of the desert took the silver plate and looked at it for a few moments. He then said,—

"This writing is neither Hebrew nor Arabic. It is Greek, and the following is its meaning: 'The image on the throne with the Crown on its head and the scepter in its hand is the likeness of Shadad the son of 'Ad, King of the desert. I ruled over a thousand thousand provinces. I rode a thousand thousand horses. A thousand thousand Kings paid me tribute. I slew a thousand thousand warriors and when the angel of death came near to me, I was powerless. My strength left me, and I was helpless. So will it ever be with all who trust in horses and chariots and rely upon the arm of flesh. Take heed, O reader, and ponder well over these words. Weigh them in thy heart and remember them.'"

"Enough," cried Solomon; "spread out my magic carpet—O Wind! lift it up and carry us back to Jerusalem. It is getting late and I will not sup to-night in Media but in the Holy City. Away."

The next second all the retinue around their King, who sat on his golden throne, were on their way to Jerusalem. In the twinkling of an eye, just as the sun began to set in the west, Solomon arrived in his capital. He entered his palace and sent for his golden pen. He dipped it into his imperishable ink and with a smile across his mouth he wrote in his scroll the story of his day's experience: "Vanity of vanities, all is vanity."

Beth Hammidrash
(ed. Jellinek, v. pp. 22–26).

V. The Magic Lamp

THERE once lived in Paris, in the good olden days, a great Jew called Rabbi Jechiel. He was a wonderful man, deeply read in the mystical lore of Israel. He was a student of the Kabbalah, or mystic science of the Hebrews. People said that he was a past master in the use of spells and magic. In fact he was supposed to be able to perform miracles by means of the formulæ current among the Kabbalists. Some people went so far as to say that he was a wizard, for strange things happened in his house. True he had many disciples who came every morning and every evening to listen to the words of wisdom that fell from his lips. Did he not have a magic lamp? He never bought oil, and in those good olden days oil was the only known means of obtaining illumination.

The story that Rabbi Jechiel had a wonderful magic lamp passed from mouth to mouth, till at last it reached the ears of the King of France. The tale sounded so extraordinary that the King determined to ascertain whether this story was mere idle rumor without any foundation, or whether the Rabbi really had a marvelous lamp. He accordingly ordered his attendants to fetch the Rabbi and to bring him to the royal presence.

As soon as Jechiel entered the salon where the King sat on his throne, he made a profound obeisance and remained standing. The King greeted him in a cordial manner and requested him to be seated. When Jechiel had obeyed the King's command he waited for the Monarch to question him.

"I have sent for you because I hear strange stories about you. You are undoubtedly a very wise man, but some of the people say that you are a magician. You are said to possess a magic lamp which you are able to burn without oil. Are you so skilled in witchcraft as to be able to do this miracle? Speak freely and have no fear. I promise to give you my protection, come what may."

Rabbi Jechiel replied,—

"Your Majesty must pardon me if I do not appear to be as frank as I might be. I cannot reveal the secrets of the Kabbalah. One versed in the Kabbalah can certainly do much more than one who is not acquainted with the ancient and wonderful teaching. Now as regards the magic lamp. I do not admit that it is a magic lamp. What I possess is a lamp the like of which your Majesty has not probably seen. This little lamp gives me sufficient illumination to suit my purpose, and true it is that I do not use any oil with this lamp."

"Now, good Rabbi, please tell me a little more about this lamp."

"Your Majesty's will is my pleasure. Now before I explain the nature of my lamp, I think it my duty to assure your Majesty that the Jewish religion is utterly opposed to magic and witchcraft. What we are, however, permitted to do—nay, we are even commanded to do it—is to study nature and to subdue it. Man is the King of all things in the universe. If my lamp can give light without oil, it is because nature was provided a substitute. People have imagined that I have this magic lamp because I do not buy oil. They do not pause to think and to ask themselves, Can we obtain illumination by any other means? The whole purpose of the Kabbalah is to teach man the duty of studying nature, and how to wrestle with it till we discover its secrets."

"I am greatly obliged to you," said the King, "and I shall be glad to see your lamp one day."

The Rabbi was then dismissed and returned to his home. The King was not entirely satisfied with Jechiel's explanation. If anything the royal curiosity was increased by what the Rabbi had said. The King determined to call on the Rabbi one evening and to take him by surprise in order to see what sort of lamp he really used.

In the good olden days of which we are speaking, there were not a few people in France who were far from being friendly to the Jews. This hostility arose from jealousy and ignorance. The Jews were steady-going people, avoiding taverns and gambling-dens, preferring to live among themselves in peace and happiness. Their religious observances were also totally unlike those of their neighbors. Church was not Synagogue, Jew was not Christian. Hence arose suspicion and misunderstanding. The city ruffians made capital of this and they were ever ready to pillage the Ghetto, or the quarter where the Jews resided. Moreover, the fame of Rabbi Jechiel, now that he had been received at court by the King, increased the excitement of the mob.

Every one wanted to see the magic lamp. The poor Rabbi had no rest. His lessons were constantly interrupted. He would begin to teach and lo! there was a knock at the door. The Rabbi would hasten to open the door and there stood before him an idle good-for-nothing asking whether he might see the magic lamp. The Rabbi replied,—

"I have no magic lamp, and even if I had I cannot spend all my days in satisfying idle curiosity."

The magic lamp soon become a source of worry to Jechiel.

"What would the Rabbi do?" asked his pupils.

"I will put a stop to this nuisance," he replied, "and you will see that we shall soon have peace."

The Rabbi discovered by means of the Kabbalistic science a method of preventing a continuance of the annoyance. He had in the floor of his study a large nail. Whenever he struck the head of the nail with the hammer, the ground outside his street-door began to give way. When a person came to vex the Rabbi and began to knock at the door, the Rabbi fetched his hammer and knocked the head of the nail in his study. The unfortunate man at the street-door felt the ground beneath his feet beginning to give way and he hastened away as quickly as his legs would carry him. The device worked so splendidly that at last the Rabbi was left alone.

One winter's night when the snow was on the ground the Rabbi was alone in his study. Outside his door stood the King with two of his attendants. The King had long determined to take the Rabbi by surprise so as to discover what sort of lamp he used. The King knocked at the door. Rabbi Jechiel paid no heed and went on reading the Zohar, the great book of the Kabbalists. Again the King knocked and this time as loudly as he could.

"Ah!" cried Jechiel, "some of my old customers have come to-night; they know that I have given my pupils a holiday and they think I have nothing better to do than to show them my lamp. Where's my hammer? Here it is"; and he picked it up, and struck the nail on its head. "Now be off, idle busy-bodies!"

Meanwhile the King and his attendants began to sink into the ground. With an effort the King managed once again to knock at the door and to cry aloud for help. Jechiel heard only the knocking, for the wind was blowing hard. Once again he seized the hammer and knocked the nail on its head, when it sprang out of the floor. This gave the Rabbi a tremendous shock.

"This can only happen," cried he in terror, "if the King or an angel were at my door."

At the same moment when the nail sprang out of the floor the ground outside the door began to rise again. Without a moment's delay Jechiel opened the street-door, and there sure enough stood the King of France with his two attendants. The King did not say a word. Jechiel fell on his face to the earth, but the King commanded him to rise up as snow was on the ground. The Rabbi obeyed and said,—

"I pray your gracious Majesty forgive me. I knew not that you were at my door. I crave your Majesty's pardon."

The King smiled and gave him his hand. The King was more than surprised, in fact he was rather terrified, as he did not know what next to expect. Such a strange experience as he had just gone through was more than enough for one evening. Here indeed was more to be wondered at than at any magic lamp.

"Well, good Rabbi," at last the King managed to say,—

"Do you not call this witchcraft and magic? Here I and my attendants have been descending into the earth as far as our hips and up again we come; what does it all mean? Please explain. I confess that I do not like such sudden shocks, and I must request you not to continue your experiments at my expense."

"That I promise most faithfully," said the Rabbi with a profound bow; "meanwhile let me beg your gracious Majesty to enter my humble home. I have a nice fire burning and your Majesty and your attendants will need warmth before you will feel at all comfortable. I will lead the way and you will soon be warm."

The King and his attendants followed Jechiel and they all entered his best room where there was a nice fire on the hearth. Jechiel gave his guests wine and cake, and once more gave expression to his deep sorrow for what had happened. He said,—

"Your Majesty will, I hope, pardon my unfortunate mistake. Had I known that your Majesty was at my door, I should have opened it even before you had knocked."

"Say no more about it," said the King. "I forgive and forget. Now tell me why did the ground under my feet fall in and rise again?"

The Rabbi told the King all about the nail, and why he had recourse to this unusual way of answering a knock at his door.

"Very clever indeed," exclaimed the King, "but I do not suppose you will tell me how you manage to work this magic nail. Well, well! I did not come out on this wretched night to inquire about your nail."

"May I ask your Majesty, then, why am I honored by your gracious presence, especially on such a night as this? I hear the wind howling outside my windows and the snow is falling fast. Your Majesty has surely some purpose in coming to my home, and as your Majesty now knows, there is some risk in gaining admission."

"Good Rabbi, I like your ready wit. It does me good to hear your clever talk."

"Your Majesty must realize that you were in danger, for had I not knocked a second time on the head of my nail, your Majesty and your attendants would have gradually sunk deeper and deeper into the ground. This is the fate that befalls all the wicked ruffians who come here merely to disturb me in my sacred studies."

"Well, good Rabbi," said the King with a smile on his face, "it is extremely lucky for me and for you that I was not swallowed up alive. At all events I am most grateful to you for saving my life. As to the purpose of my midnight visit to you, let me tell you at once why I am here. You will remember when you came to my palace I asked you whether you had a magic lamp. You told me that you had a lamp which required no oil, but you denied that it was a magic lamp. Not only have I heard so much about your magical powers, I have to-night experienced how powerful your skill is in witchcraft. I have come to see your lamp and I now ask you to show it to me."

"With pleasure. Will your Majesty be good enough to follow me and I will show you the lamp, which I keep in my small sitting-room?"

They entered the little room and on the table in the center of the room there was a marvelous little lamp.

The King looked at it and said: "Wonderful! there is no oil here." The lamp was a crystal mortar full of phosphorus which had been melted some years previously in a few drops of olive-oil.

Naturally as this was the only source of illumination in

the dark room it emitted light enough to enable one to see the different objects in the room.

"This is truly wonderful," exclaimed the King.

"Do not be astonished at this," said Jechiel. "God has given us various means of obtaining light without combustion. Have you never heard of plants that evolve light? Well, there are such plants. Has your Majesty never heard of the luminosity of decaying wood? There are even insects, such as the glow-worm and other beetles, which throw off light. Fish and other living things, such as sea pens, are also luminous. The same can be said of a number of mineral substances, such as fluor-spar and calcium. Then again we have lightning. Truly knowledge is light, and the laws of God are a lamp on the way of life."

The King was astounded to hear such marvelous wisdom from a Jew. He had never heard anything like it in all his life. Not one of his counselors had ever spoken of nature and her secrets in a similar strain.

"I thank you ever so much for all you have taught me. I have been well repaid for coming to see you. Henceforth you will be one of my counselors of state and I hope you will also be my personal friend. You will live in a suite of rooms in my palace and you will be able to continue your studies undisturbed. Now accept this ring as a token of my esteem."

The King took from his finger a beautiful ring, which he placed on the Rabbi's finger. Then the King departed, greatly pleased with all that he had seen and heard.

Rabbi Jechiel was now established at court. He was the King's favorite. He even taught the King some of the secrets of alchemy. All this aroused the jealousy of the other courtiers and counselors. One day some of them remarked to the King,—

"We do not understand how your Majesty can tolerate a Jew living in your palace. You do not know the nature of a Jew. He is so unlike a Christian. It will surprise your Majesty to learn that he actually despises you, and of course all of us."

"How dare you say this?" cried the King in warmth.

"We can prove it, if your Majesty would but let us do so," said they.

"How so?"

"If your Majesty would give him a glass of wine of which you have tasted but one drop, he will indignantly refuse to empty the glass, he would not even drink a drop. He is so proud and vain. Is the conduct of such a man not a direct insult to your gracious Majesty and to the Kingdom of France?"

The King held his peace.

Next day when the Rabbi came to visit the King, all the counselors and courtiers were also in attendance.

"Give me a glass of wine," cried the King, "and also a little fruit, for I feel somewhat faint."

The page brought the wine and the fruit on a golden salver. The King ate the fruit and sipped the sparkling wine. Then turning to the Rabbi, who sat near the throne, he said in a loud voice so that all present might hear,—

"Jechiel, my friend! this is most excellent wine; I have just tasted it, but I do not feel faint now, for the fruit has quite revived me. Here, drink the wine whilst I rinse my hands. It would be such a pity to waste it, and to whom could I give it with more pleasure than to you, my friend and companion."

The courtiers and counselors listened with strained ears to every word, and they now looked at Jechiel to see what he would do.

The Jew put forth his hand and took the glass from the King's hand. He then put it down on a little table at his side. He arose from his seat and said,—

"May I crave your Majesty's indulgence? At the moment I do not care to take wine. I have a good reason. I must keep my head cool, for your Majesty has to discuss with me urgent matters of state. But do not think I am not fully sensible of the great honor which your Majesty is good enough to confer upon me in asking me to drink the wine which you find so excellent. I promise, however, before I take my leave this morning to drink even more than your Majesty proposes."

The listeners could hardly believe their ears.

"What," thought they, "will the Jew drink with Christians?"

When the King had rinsed his fingers with rose water in a golden bowl, the Rabbi arose and took the bowl from the page and laid it beside the glass of wine.

"What's that for?" exclaimed the King in surprise.

The Rabbi arose, and taking hold of the golden bowl said in a fearless voice,—

"With your gracious Majesty's permission I will now drink this water which has just been used by you, my King and friend. I may drink this water, for the hands of a good and just King are always clean, and therefore the water is as fresh as when it was brought to your Majesty. My religion permits me to drink water but not wine. The wine is forbidden because it very often happens that wine used by Kings is also used by priests for religious purposes." Whereupon to the great surprise of all present Jechiel drank the rose water and resumed his seat.

The wise King saw all this and understood.

"Now I know," cried he, "how greatly this good Jew loves me, and I rejoice to think that he loves his God and his religion with all his heart. Happy am I to have such a friend; would that all my servants were as zealous and as faithful."

Shalsheleth Hakkabalah
(ed. Amsterdam, 1697 p. 44b).

VI. Chanina and the Angels

WHILST the Temple was still standing it was the custom of all the Jews to bring their sacrifices and gifts to Jerusalem. Rich and poor vied with one another in bringing offerings to the Holy House of God. Now there was a very poor man named Chanina who lived far away from the Holy City. In his own town he saw his fellow townsmen preparing themselves for their pilgrimage to Zion where the Temple was. Each one had an offering or present and he alone had nothing. He asked himself: "What can I find worthy of God's acceptance?"

He looked around in his humble home, but he could not find anything of value.

"All my neighbors," said he to himself, "will set out next week for Jerusalem taking their offerings with them and I, alas! will appear before the Lord empty-handed. This will not do, it must not be."

He then betook himself to the stone quarries near the town where he lived. He gazed around and saw a huge block of marble which had been placed on the rubbish heap, because its surface was too rough for polishing. He resolved to make its surface smooth, be the trouble never so great. From sunrise till sunset he worked. At last his patience and labor were rewarded. The surface of the stone became smooth and fit for polishing.

When this task was accomplished, Chanina rejoiced greatly.

"Now," he exclaimed, "this shall be my gift to God's

Temple. The difficulty which now confronts me is, How am I to get this beautiful block to Jerusalem? I vow to give it to God's service and it must be taken to the Temple."

He returned to his town to look for carriers. He found a dozen men who could easily transport it. He asked them whether they would take the marble to the Holy City. They replied,—

"We will do what you want, if you pay us."

"Tell me, good friends, how much do you want?"

"One hundred golden coins."

"Where can I find such an immense sum of money? See," cried he, "this is all I possess; let me count. One, two, three, four, five pence. This is my total fortune. If you will trust me and should kind Providence help me to earn money, I will gladly pay you all you demand. Now you are going to Jerusalem for the Festival and you might at the same time transport this marble, which I have vowed to give to the Sanctuary."

They laughed at him, as though he were joking, and went their way, leaving him alone. After a while he saw an old man coming along. When they met the stranger greeted him and said,—

"What a fine block of marble! Do you know to whom it belongs?"

"I found it here some days ago cast on the rubbish heap. I have polished its surface and I have vowed to give it to the Temple."

"You have done well, my son. How will you have it removed to the Holy City?"

"That is just the difficulty which is troubling me at the present moment."

"Well, perhaps I can help you. I have five servants yonder. If you will lend a hand, I think we can transport it."

"Most gladly will I do as you say, and in addition I will pay you five pence, all I possess at present."

"So be it."

At that moment five tall men came forward and at once placed their hands on the marble. As in a blinding storm they rushed along, carried by the huge block, and before many seconds had passed Chanina found himself beside the marble in the Temple Court. He rubbed his eyes, for he thought that he was dreaming, but when he saw the priests and the Levites coming towards him he knew that he was wide awake.

"The Lord be with thee, O Chanina," they cried.

"May the Lord bless you!" he answered.

He then turned round to look for the old man and his five men, but they had vanished. He wanted to give them the five pence which he had promised to pay. He then asked the priests to accept the marble as his gift for the coming festival, and he also handed to them the five pence, asking them to distribute the money to the poor. With great joy in his heart he thanked God for the miracle which had befallen him. He said to himself,—

"I believe the old man was Elijah the prophet, and the five men with him were ministering angels. The wonders of the Lord never cease."

Chanina felt his coat pressing rather heavily on his shoulders. He put his hands into his pockets, and he was amazed to find them full of golden coins. He rejoiced at this fresh token of Heaven's favor, and when he returned home he had sufficient money to spend his days in comfort.

Canticles Rabbah, Canticles i. i.

VII. The Wonderful Slave

THERE was once upon a time a very poor man who had a wife and five children. It happened one day that there was no food in the house. The wife told her husband that she had nothing to give the children.

"And I am sorry to say," he cried, "I haven't a penny. I cannot find any work and I don't know what will become of us. God help us, I cannot see any way out of our misfortune."

"Cheer up, dear husband; go down to the market-place and perhaps you will be in luck's way and find some job. You are no fool, and you often say, 'God neither slumbers nor sleeps' but watches over all of us."

"To whom can I turn when I get there? I don't know a soul there. As you know we haven't a relative in the town, and as for friends, well we know what they are worth. When we had money we had plenty of friends, but when we lost our wealth we also lost our friends."

"There is, good husband, still one Friend left."

"You mean the good God?"

"Of course I do. Now don't waste time, for we are all starving; go to the market-place and see what happens."

Away he went. Meanwhile the poor children came to their mother and cried for bread. This distressed her very much. She wept and prayed to God to help them in their hour of need.

When the poor man reached the market-place he stood still for a few minutes looking around. It was full of people, hurrying hither and thither. Not a soul did the unfortunate man recognize. Passers-by just looked at him, and he felt very lonely and sad. He walked across the market-place and sat down behind some bundles of hay, where he would be hidden from view. He began to pray, saying,—

"Lord of the Universe! Thou knowest that I have neither relative nor friend to whom I can go and pour out my heart's troubles. Thou seest the dire poverty and distress which have befallen my family. My only hope is in Thee; take pity upon us, not for my sake, but for the sake of my poor wife and helpless children. I beseech Thee send us Thy help, or if it seem good in Thine eyes let us die, for we know neither peace nor rest."

The man then arose and was somewhat taken aback to see a young man at his side. The stranger was Elijah the prophet, who is like the good fairy in the story-books. His mission is to comfort all who are in trouble. He champions those who cannot find any one to help them. He defends lost causes and helps all those who need succor. He reclaims the lost and seeks those who stray from the highway of life through no default on their part. He is ever moved by a passion of pity and hastens to the side of all who have faith in God, even when all else fails.

"Good-day, good friend," cries Elijah; "peace be unto you."

"Peace be unto you also," replies the poor man.

"Why are you so downcast, what's your trouble?"

"How can you help me?"

"I certainly cannot help you if you do not tell me why you look so forlorn and miserable. Have you lost anything?"

"Yes, I have lost everything."

"Explain, please; do not hesitate to confide in me. You can really trust me."

"Good stranger, since you speak so kindly I will trust you and tell you all about my misfortunes. I have at home a dear wife and five sweet children. They are all starving. There is not a crust in the house. I am penniless and out of work. I will gladly do anything if I can find any one who will employ me. My will is good and no toil will be too hard or too much for me. If you would really help me, find me work or recommend me to some one to give me employment."

Elijah took hold of the man's hand and said,—

"I think I can do something better for you than you suggest. I will do the work for you which will enable you and your dear family to live in comfort. Do not worry and just do what I tell you."

"What do you wish me to do?"

"We will go at once to the slave market, which adjoins this market. When we get there you are to offer me for sale as a slave. The money you will get for my purchase shall be yours. Henceforth you and your family will know want no more."

"How could I do such a thing as you suggest? You are not my slave. You are a perfect stranger, and it would be far more reasonable to reverse the proposition. We will go to the slave market and you shall offer me for sale. Whatever I am worth will suffice to keep my poor wife and children from starvation. Come, let us do as I say, and I shall be ever so grateful to you for obliging me in this way."

"No, no," cried Elijah, "you are to sell me as your slave, and within twenty-four hours you will see me again. When you receive the money from the buyer in the market, do not forget to give me a coin. You do not know who I am. Continue to trust in God and follow my instructions. I assure you all will be well and you will be happy and contented. Now for the slave market."

They came there and all the buyers thought that the poor man was the slave and the stranger his master. They were surprised to hear the poor man call out in a bold voice,—

"I have here a most valuable slave for sale."

The bidders began to make offers. At that moment one of the Princes of the King of the land passed by, and when he saw Elijah he returned and resolved to buy such a noble-looking slave for the King his master. The bidding went on and the Prince offered eighty pieces of gold. Whereupon Elijah whispered to his poor friend,—

"Sell me now to this bidder: do not accept a higher price."

He did just as Elijah told him and accepted the eighty pieces of gold and immediately gave one to his generous benefactor. The latter returned it, saying,—

"Now take this coin and live by means of its blessing; it will enable you and all your family to exist in comfort. Want and poverty shall never again trouble you all the days of your life. We will now part, and I wish you God's blessing."

The poor man thanked Elijah with tears in his eyes. He said,—

"I grieve to think you should allow yourself to become a slave just to help me and my family. I have done just as you told me because I seem to feel that you are wiser than I am. You said I should see you again within twenty-four hours. I do not see how that will be possible now that you are a slave."

"You will see me within the appointed time; till then farewell."

Elijah then went away, following his new master. The fortunate poor man hastened home after he had bought food in the market. When he reached his home he found his children and his wife famished with hunger. He spread the excellent food which he had brought with him upon the table and called his dear ones to see what the good God had given them. They ran to their usual seats at table and could hardly believe their eyes. For two days they had seen no food, and now the table was loaded with fish and bread, cake and fruit. They all said the Grace before eating bread and enjoyed their meal more than they had ever done in all their life. They recited the Grace after meals with gratitude in their hearts. Now a strange thing struck all at table. In spite of all they had eaten, and that was not by any means a small quantity, there was enough food left for a week's supply. This made them all the happier, and they praised God for His never-ending mercies.

"Now please," said the wife to her husband, "tell me how did you manage to obtain all this beautiful food? It is all so good and there is so much of it. I am dying to know what happened to you in the market-place. I know you have not obtained all this food by theft. It was I who urged you to go to the market-place, for I felt convinced that the good God would help us in our terrible misfortune."

He told her all that had happened to him. He described how the stranger came to him in the market-place and how he had allowed himself to be sold as a slave.

"This is a marvelous slice of luck," she cried.

"But it is not all."

He related how he had given the stranger one piece of gold and how it had been returned. The wonderful words which the stranger had said when he returned the piece of gold were also retold. Happiness filled the hearts of the good man and his wife. Henceforth wealth and prosperity never forsook them. They were spared all further worldly cares and troubles.

Meanwhile the Prince had brought his new slave before the King his master. The latter had long planned in his mind to build a wonderful palace in a wood adjoining his capital. He had already commenced the building. The foundation was completely finished. He had hired very many slaves to carry wood, stone and other material required for its construction. When Elijah came before the King he was asked,—

"What is your trade?"

"I am an architect and also a practical builder."

"Excellent!" exclaimed the King in great joy; "it is my ardent desire to complete the building of my palace in the wood near by. My architect died six months ago, and since then the work seems to make no progress. It must be built according to my wishes. There must be so and so many stories with so and so many rooms on each floor."

He then proceeded to tell him exactly what his wishes were. When he had finished Elijah remarked,—

"I will endeavor to carry out your Majesty's plan exactly as you have explained. May I ask, when is the building to be finished?"

"If the building could be erected within twelve months I should be exceedingly happy. If you achieve this result I will give you your freedom and present you with a handsome gift."

"I will do my best," replied Elijah; "and now may I ask your Majesty to order your slaves to recommence even at this very hour their tasks. There are yet four hours before sundown. The labor is great and the time is short."

The King forthwith ordered his chamberlain to do as Elijah had requested. The slave architect went to the wood and watched the slaves carrying brick and mortar. At sundown they ceased their labor and went home. Elijah remained alone. He arose and prayed to God asking Him to cause the palace to be built there and then even as the King desired. The prayer of the faithful prophet was heard by the Great Architect of the Universe, who sent down myriads of His ministering angels to complete the building. The work was soon done, every detail was carefully attended to by the heavenly builders. Before sunrise next day the wonderful palace stood complete. Elijah was well satisfied and went on his way. He was seen no more in the King's city.

At daybreak the people heard from the slaves who had gone to continue their tasks that the palace had been miraculously built overnight. The extraordinary news was at once communicated to the King. He went immediately to the wood to see the miracle. Needless to say he was mightily pleased with everything he saw. He rejoiced to see the wish of his heart realized in such a brief space of time. Everything was done in accordance with his plan. There was not a single defect to be seen.

"Bring me," he cried, "the marvelous slave who has

performed the greatest miracle ever heard of in my kingdom."

The servants of the King searched everywhere for the slave, but he was not to be found. This was reported to the King, who remarked,—"This is another miracle."

He now saw that the slave was no ordinary one. "I believe," he added, "that the slave was an angel."

Meanwhile Elijah had gone to visit the man whom he had befriended. When the latter saw him he cried,—

"You have indeed come to see me within the twenty-four hours as you promised. Tell me, good friend, who are you?"

"I am Elijah the prophet."

"What happened when you came before the King?"

"He wanted a beautiful palace to be built within twelve months. God hearkened to my prayer and within twelve hours the palace was erected."

"This is all very wonderful."

"Naturally; whatever God does is marvelous. I assumed the rôle of a slave, and as a good price had been paid for my services, I determined to give good value in return. The palace which has been built through my prayer is, of course, worth more than a thousand times the money paid to you."

"How, saintly Elijah, Man of God, can I repay you? You have saved my life and the lives of my wife and children."

"You can repay me by living a good life, ever helping all God's children in distress."

"This I faithfully promise to do."

The next moment Elijah had vanished, leaving the happy man full of joy and gratitude in his heart.

Beth Hammidrash (ed. Jellinek, v. pp. 140f.); see
also *Baer's Hebrew Prayer Book* (pp. 316f.).

VIII. About Leviathan, King of the Fish

O N the left bank of the Jordan lived a pious old man and his only son. The father was a fisherman and caught sufficient fish to provide for the modest needs of his son and himself. He was accustomed every day after he had drawn in his net to throw a basketful of bread to the fish. He would say,—

"These little fish feed me and my son, and I in return must feed those that are left in the river."

One day it rained so heavily while he was fishing that he was drenched to the skin. He felt cold and ill and kept in bed next day. Towards evening he became very feverish, and calling his son to his bedside he said,—

"Dear son Samuel, I fear I shall not get rid of my cold. I shall soon trouble you no longer. You have been a very good and loving son and I bless you. I am so sorry I cannot leave you any fortune. Continue your studies of our Holy Bible. I give you my old net as your heritage. If you would prosper continue to observe my custom of feeding the fish. Stand, even as I have been wont to do for so many years, opposite our house on the bank of the river. Do not throw the bread to the fish before you have withdrawn the net. It is not fair to throw in the bread, and when the hungry fish come for their food to swoop down upon them and fill your net with them. First catch your fish, then feed the rest. You will one day understand the saying of our wise King Solomon: 'Cast thy bread upon the face of the waters, and after many days thou wilt find it again.'[1]"

---

1. Eccles. xi. 1.

"Dearest father! do not think you will not get well again. I will look after you and by the help of the Almighty you will soon be about again."

"Good son! I fear not. My days are numbered and I shall soon sleep in the dust. I again bless you if you promise to carry out my wish."

"Of course I promise. Have no fear. I will faithfully keep my promise just because it is your wish."

That same night the good old man slept into death, for the angel of God kissed his lips. He was buried by his sorrowing son who loved him so truly. Every day Samuel went to the bank of the river to throw in his net. He stood just where his father used to stand. After he had drawn in his net, he took out of his basket handfuls of fresh white bread which he threw into the river. He was very much surprised to find that there was always a very large fish that appeared as soon as the bread reached the water. This fish managed to eat up very quickly the larger portion of the bread. Consequently there was very little left for the small fish. Moreover if one of the latter happened to be in the way of the large fish, the unfortunate little thing received a nasty knock in the back from the heavy tail of the greedy monster. This grieved Samuel, but what was he to do? The same thing happened every day since the burial of his dear father.

The more the big fish ate the larger it grew. This made the little ones fear it all the more.

"What's to be done?" said the latter one day, when they saw the greedy fish devour every scrap of bread thrown into the water by their kind-hearted friend. After very many prolonged discussions they resolved to send three of their wisest brethren as a deputation to Leviathan, King of the fish.

"Let his gracious Majesty," said they, "hear our just complaint, and he will know how to rectify our grievance. He will bring the horrid offender to book. It's high time the fat old fish had his greedy head chopped off by the public executioner. He will be a terrible example to all fish to be more careful and not to be greedy and selfish. He is a perfect disgrace to rob us of our lovely white bread."

Away the deputation swam till they came to the palace of King Leviathan, right at the bottom of the sea. It was such a marvelous palace, built of mother-of-pearl and corals. The King's body-guard were wonderful fish; their scales were luminous and they could be seen miles and miles away. When the three little fish knocked at the palace door, they were at once admitted; and when they said that they were a deputation to his Majesty they were immediately ushered into the royal presence. Directly King Leviathan saw them he began to smile and wanted to laugh in their face. He managed, however, to exercise just sufficient self-control so as not to betray his intense amusement.

"Well, little children! where do you come from?"

"O great and mighty King, we come from the Jordan."

"Where's that?"

"Where Jericho is."

"What's wrong that brings you all the way from Jericho?"

"We will tell your Majesty if you will listen to our tale. We live near the bank of the famous river Jordan. Every day a most kind-hearted man comes to bring us fresh white bread. He breaks it up into ever so many little pieces, so that every one of us shall have something to eat. Now near our homes lives a very big fish. As soon as the bread reaches the water, there he is with his big gaping mouth and he swallows up the lot. We are simply robbed of our daily bread by this wicked old fish. If your Majesty will not intervene to put an end to his tricks, he will at last become as big and as powerful as your Majesty. Would you like that? We should not, and we therefore most humbly beseech your Majesty to protect us and to punish the common enemy."

"We thank you for your concern and loyalty to our royal person. We do not approve of one of our subjects daring to become as big and as powerful as we are. Go, good body-guard, and accompany these three little fish to their home in the Jordan and see that our orders are obeyed. Now, little fish, listen to our commands. When you reach the Jordan burrow out the ground under the place where the nice man stands when he throws his bread into the water. Tell your enemy, the large and fat fish, to help you also in doing this work. When the kind man comes the next day to throw his bread into the water, the ground will give way, and he will fall into the water. Then my body-guard will catch him and bring him to our royal presence. When we see him, we will hear what he has to say. Of course the greedy fat fish is also to be present when we examine the nice man. Now, little children, do you understand?"

"Of course we do, and we thank your gracious Majesty for your kindness in taking such an interest in our affairs. We will do exactly as we have been commanded and we will soon return with our friend, the good man, and our enemy, the greedy fat fish. Farewell! Long live your Majesty!"

"Farewell, little children."

The little fish were mightily pleased with their audience with their mighty King.

"Wasn't he most charming?" said they to one another. Away they swam, accompanied by the royal body-guard.

"What will the greedy monster say," they whispered, "when he sees us with such a fine body-guard? He will be mad with jealousy. How he will splash when we give him the King's order to assist us in our work and to return with us to the palace!"

When they reached home they called on their enemy and told him all that the King had commanded. He rolled his eyes and opened his enormous mouth as though he would swallow them up alive, and then he said,—

"His Majesty's orders shall be obeyed."

The greedy fish did not like this turn of affairs at all. The whole business displeased him very much. In fact, it made him feel very ill and despondent.

"Where shall I now find my daily bread? It was so easy to come down here every morning and to find all I needed thrown into my mouth. So much to eat and so little to do. I wonder when I shall again eat such beautiful and delicious bread, fit for old Leviathan himself. These wretched little fish have added insult to injury by their audacity in asking King Leviathan to order me to assist them in the wicked task of undermining the ground whereon my charming friend stands when he throws his lovely bread to me. Talk about justice, is this not murder? He is bound to fall into the water. He will sink and be drowned like a rat. I wish I could save him, but I fear I must obey the King's orders. I wonder what the royal body-guard are doing here? I do not like to ask them any questions. They always say,—'Wait and see'—a very safe rule in the kingdom of the sea."

Without any further delay all the little fish, together with the large one and the body-guard, swam to the place where the kind man was accustomed to stand. They burrowed for all they were worth and never ceased till the royal body-guard cried out: "Enough."

Next morning when the good man came with his net on one shoulder, and in his hand the large basket full of bread, he at once took up his position on his usual spot. When lo! the ground beneath his feet gave way and he was thrown into the Jordan, net and all. At that moment the large fish opened his enormous mouth and swallowed up the man. The body-guard were very vexed at this mishap, but they merely told the fat fish that they were now to swim to King Leviathan's palace. The little fish followed, for they were very curious to know what would happen at the King's court.

When they came to the palace the doors were opened to admit them and they all entered. King Leviathan was sitting on his throne with his golden crown on his head and all his courtiers were around him. The large fish came straight before the King and said,—

"I have been as quick as I possibly could in obeying the

orders of your gracious Majesty. I have brought with me the man whom you desire to see. Let me tell your Majesty that he is one in a million; he is so kind-hearted. He feeds your Majesty's subjects, and I do hope your Majesty will not suffer any harm to befall such a splendid man. I have now much pleasure in presenting him to your Majesty."

He thereupon disgorged the poor fellow, who felt more dead than alive. His terrible experience had almost frightened him out of his wits. He thought that his last moment in life was at hand when he saw King Leviathan glide off his throne and come nearer and nearer to him. The King's jaws were apart and before the poor fellow could count "one"—he was right in the Leviathan's mouth and down into his inside. Thereupon Leviathan closed his jaws with a terrific bang that made the ocean tremble.

Now the poor man thought of his dear father's blessing and wondered what was coming next. All of a sudden he heard these words:

"I welcome you, son of the children of men; your presence here is most heartily and cordially welcome. I know just a little about nice human beings. It was my great pleasure some long time ago to entertain Jonah, when he came down here on a short visit. I had the privilege of showing him my palace and some of my treasures. I have since been told that he returned to earth, all the better for his visit down here. He had been sent to the bottom of the sea in order to learn the lesson of obedience. You need have no fear. Just answer my questions and I promise to deal kindly with you, for you are now my guest. It was at my special order that you were brought here. Now tell me, Why do you daily throw bread to my subjects, the fish? What is your object and what is your motive in doing this kind and thoughtful act?"

Samuel replied: "One thought only filled my heart and soul, and that was to obey my dying father's last injunction. On his death-bed he commanded me to go daily to the bank of the Jordan to throw a basketful of nice fresh white bread into the river for the hungry fish. I have done this every day since my dear father's burial. I may tell you that my good father also did the same every day of his life."

"Now tell me," asked Leviathan, "what do you do for your living?"

"I am a poor fisherman, even as my dear father was before me."

"Where do you live?"

"In a little house not far from Jericho on the Jordan. You have surely heard of Jericho. It had mighty walls, and when God's priests blew their trumpets the walls fell down flat on the ground."

"I had heard thereof. I believe the leader of the Israelites who conquered Jericho was Joshua."

"Yes, that is so."

"I have heard of Joshua in another connection. When he was quite a little boy he was swallowed by a whale, and as you well know, he did not perish. Did your father tell you anything else?"

"Yes, he said that if I feed the fish his blessing would always rest on me. Now I fear I have reaped the opposite to a blessing."

"Don't say that, please," said Leviathan in a very gentle voice. "We fish are very sensitive, we never forget a kind action. You and your father have always loved my subjects, and I their King will not prove myself to be ungrateful. I tell my little children, for thus I call my fish, that we are made by God to be a blessing even as all things which He has made are intended to serve the same purpose. To show you how much I appreciate your obedience to your dear father and your kindness, I will teach you the language of birds and beasts. I will also carry you immediately to the bank of the Jordan, not very far from your home. You will have but one hour's walk in order to reach your house."

Leviathan immediately carried out his promises. He taught Samuel the language of beasts and birds and brought him to the bank of the Jordan. Samuel thanked the kind-hearted monarch of the deep and rejoiced to tread the face of mother earth once again. He stood still for a few moments to gaze around. He could not but enjoy the beauty of the scene, the silver waters of the Jordan, the green grass on the banks, the play of light in the heavens, the song of the birds, the scent of the roses, the sound of nature awake and alert. He recalled the wonderful vision of the deep and the marvelous sights he had seen. He was glad, supremely glad, to breathe the sweet air, and his heart was full of gratitude to God. He suddenly felt very giddy. He had been fasting all the while he had been in the water, and this together with the lack of fresh air affected him for the moment. He put himself to rest awhile under a large tree. He closed his eyes for a few seconds and then opened them again, for the giddiness had passed. He sat still thinking of his strange experiences. He was suddenly startled to hear a little crow say to a large one at its side,—

"Look, father! I am going to enjoy myself now by eating the eyes of that man on the ground."

Samuel looked up and saw two crows sitting on a bough just over his head. He listened and heard the larger bird say,—

"Do no such thing, the man is probably alive."

"No, father, he is dead, for his eyes were shut."

"Well, they are open now, and he is looking at us. You always think you must have everything you fancy. Listen to your old father, I advise you to stay where you are. If you try to peck out his eyes, he will catch hold of you and kill you. Be wise and do not look for trouble."

Samuel understood the whole conversation, not a word escaped him. He felt very thankful to King Leviathan for the precious knowledge he had imparted to him. He thought that the little crow would follow his father's advice. He listened and then heard the little bird say,—

"I am going to eat the eyes of that man, even if I risk my life in the attempt."

Away it flew and came nearer and nearer to Samuel. No

sooner had it placed its little feet upon his forehead than he caught hold of it in his hand. He then sat up, intending to twist its neck for being so disobedient to its father. The old crow saw this and flew to the ground and turning to the little bird said,—

"It would just serve you right, you wicked and disobedient child. You never will listen to me when I tell you what you should do and what you should not do."

The old bird then turned to Samuel and said,—

"If you spare my naughty child's life, I will give you a great treasure, which will make you as rich as King Herod. You will always be wealthy and you will be able to enjoy life."

"I agree," said Samuel, "to do as you say, if you tell me where the treasure is to be found. As soon as I see it, I will set your child free."

"The treasure," rejoined the crow, "is at the foot of this tree, it lies but a few inches beneath the ground. Remove the soil and you will see the treasure."

Samuel looked about for a piece of wood, and when he found it, he scraped away the earth at the foot of the tree. His labor was soon rewarded, for he saw a large box. He opened it and found it full of gold coins. His joy was indeed great. "Now I know," said he to himself, "why King Leviathan cast me ashore at this spot. I guess he knew all about the treasure."

He released the crow and told it to obey its old father in future. The two birds flew away, saying to each other, "What a lucky escape."

Samuel filled his pockets with the gold coin. He closed the box and covered it up with the soil. He then went home. He returned next day to the tree with a wheelbarrow upon which he intended to put the box with the gold. He did this and was now a rich man. His father's blessing had indeed brought him his wealth and his knowledge of the language of birds and beasts. He was very thankful to God for all these favors. He continued to feed the fish, and he was so glad to see that the little ones were no longer robbed of their share by the greedy big fish. Samuel lived a good and happy life, feeding and helping the poor and the unfortunate. He was beloved and honored throughout the land and ended his days in comfort and peace.

Maàseh Book (*Chap Book*), ed. Wilmersdorf.
No. 133.

IX. The Demon's Marriage

L ONG, long ago, in quite the olden time, there lived a King who had an only daughter. The monarch was very wealthy and he was exceedingly proud of being so rich. To be sure, he had much more money than he deserved to have. He thought more about money than about anything else. He was also haughty because he wore a crown. He listened to silly people who told him that his blood was blue, because he was a King. "Like father, like child," says an old proverb, and the Princess was also very proud. She loved money, and thought herself better than everybody else.

When a poor noble Prince came to woo her, she would refuse to listen to his heart's cry; telling him that his rank was not good enough, or that his money was far too little for her ideas. In fact, she thought that money was the only thing worth having in life. Her father, instead of rebuking her and correcting her, encouraged her to look for rank and wealth as the first qualifications in any suitor. In fact, he used to say that he would never allow her to marry any one unless he happened to be a Prince who had as much money as he had.

Many suitors came to win her hand, but she rejected them. Some of these men were noble and good men; their only fault was their poverty. One day when she was celebrating her twenty-third birthday her father said to her,—

"I do wish, dear daughter, that Princes who are beggars would keep away from our court."

"To be sure, dear father, I quite agree. I have no patience with poor people who think of marrying me for the sake of my wealth."

Not long after this conversation there appeared in the courtyard of the palace a handsome young fellow dressed like a Prince in silk and velvet. His sword was of gold, and he had diamonds in the buckles of his shoes. He knocked at the palace door and when it was opened he asked to see the King. He was admitted and conducted at once to the royal presence. He advanced towards the throne whereon the King sat, and, after bowing in a very stately fashion, exclaimed,—

"May your gracious Majesty live long and live well! I am a Prince with very blue blood; my pedigree is unparalleled, I can assure you. I have come to ask your Majesty's permission to woo your lovely daughter. I am longing to see her, for I hear that she is the most beautiful Princess in all the world. The fame of her beauty has reached my father's realm, and I now ask you to allow me to see her."

"Well, noble Prince, I think I can allow you to see her. Like all wise Princesses, she has made up her mind to be uninfluenced in her love affairs. I cannot help you. What I will do, however, is to second your efforts, if my daughter seems favorably disposed towards you."

He then ordered his chamberlain to request the Princess to come to the throne-room.

"Tell her royal highness," he added, "that a most noble Prince is being received in audience and desires to make her royal highness' acquaintance."

After a few minutes' interval, the Princess entered the throne-room and sat on a chair of state beside her father. She looked very beautiful and her court jewels added to her adornment.

"Permit me to greet your royal highness," said the visitor, "and will you favor me by accepting this small gift which I have brought from my royal father."

He then gave her a gold casket full of brilliants and pearls. There were rings and bracelets set with glistening diamonds and rubies. She gazed for some time at the wonderful sight, and when she had feasted her eyes sufficiently she cried aloud,—

"Look, father dear! See what a wonderful gift this charming Prince has brought me. Never before did I receive such a lovely present. I cannot find words to thank the Prince."

"Truly wonderful and right royal is the gift," said the King, and turning to his daughter he said: "Now leave us."

"Now may I speak?" said the Prince with a smile on his face. "I have come to win the hand and heart of your lovely daughter. I am indeed so much in love with her that I venture to ask you to consent to my endeavor to win her love. I know you will not allow her to wed a poor Prince. I feel sure that I can satisfy you that I am not only as wealthy as your Majesty, but I can claim to possess more money than can be found in your kingdom. I am, of course, of noble descent as I have already mentioned. My father rules a great kingdom and I am the heir-apparent."

"By all appearances," observed the King, "your royal highness seems to be a very wealthy and noble Prince. I must confess that I have been agreeably surprised by your kindness in giving my daughter such a magnificent present."

"Oh, your Majesty!" said the Prince, "pray do not mention this again. It was a mere bagatelle compared with the jewels I have with me here in my apartments. If your Majesty will honor me by accompanying me to my rooms I will be able to show your Majesty a small portion of my wealth. I do not like to boast, but I must tell you that I have with me antique and precious gems of greater value than all the crown jewels of your Majesty. Such things as I possess your Majesty has never seen. All this is as nothing compared with the wealth in my castles and palace at home. All this fortune awaits my future wife. I hope it will be your daughter. Have I your consent?"

"What is the name of your father's kingdom, and what is your own name?"

"I am called Prince Daring and my father's realm is called the Kingdom of Delight; it is situated far away beyond the hills, across the sea. Probably in such a small kingdom as this your Majesty has never heard of this realm. Do not your subjects say, 'The proof of the pudding is in the eating'? Here I am, at all events, and you can judge what sort of Prince I am. Your own eyes shall have abundant proof as to my enormous wealth. I imagine your experience tells you that you can recognize in me the exterior of a Prince the like of whom you have rarely seen at your court. Kindly tell me now whether I am acceptable to your Majesty as a future son-in-law."

"I will give my decision when I have seen your treasures."

"Will your Majesty accompany me now to my rooms?"

"We will go at once."

The King went with the Prince to his lodging, which was in one of the best hotels in the city. The King was astounded to see in one of the rooms more gold, silver, jewels, and precious material than he had ever seen in all his life.

"Well, I never," observed the King, "expected to see such wealth and treasure; you must be a hundred times richer than I am. Of course you have my consent to wed my sweet daughter. I am sure you will make a very good son-in-law."

They then returned to the palace. The King sent for the Princess and told her that he quite approved of the Prince as her future husband. The Princess with a blush on her face said,—

"I am quite happy to be the bride of such a noble Prince whose wealth will enable us to be happy and to enjoy life in a manner becoming our rank."

"Of that there can be no doubt," said the King.

"Yes, you shall have as much money as you want, sweet Princess," said the Prince.

"I shall realize my dream of having heaps and heaps of money, amusement will make me so happy," said the Princess with joy in her eyes.

The Prince then placed a lovely diamond engagement ring on the finger of the Princess, saying: "With this ring do I betroth thee unto me." He then kissed her. But she seemed to be chilled by his cold lips and she trembled for a second. Her father wished her joy and kissed her. The King summoned his courtiers and told of his daughter's engagement. The happy bridal couple received the congratulations of the entire court. Heralds were sent to all parts of the kingdom to proclaim the good news. The people rejoiced when they heard that the Princess had at last found a husband.

Elaborate preparations for the royal wedding were at once taken in hand. The marriage was fixed to take place in a week's time. All the nobles and the rich merchants were invited to witness the function and to attend the State ball which was to follow the happy event. The banquet after the marriage ceremony was truly royal. The best of everything was provided in abundance. The choicest wines were taken from the royal cellars. The King determined to make an effort in order to impress his rich son-in-law. He spared no expense to provide a magnificent feast, and he succeeded so well that all his guests were surprised and delighted.

After the first week of their married life, the Prince came to his father-in-law and said,—

"Beloved father of my wife! I crave your Majesty's permission to return to my own land and home with my dear wife. I promised my good father that I should not be absent from his court for more than twenty days. I have spent fourteen days here as your guest and I took three days to come here and I need three days for the return journey. My time is now up. I dare not disappoint the King my father lest he be angry with me and your daughter. It would never do for my sweet wife to meet her father-in-law in one of his dreadful tempers. He is liable to fits of wicked temper, and if I am not greatly mistaken most monarchs are subject to the same trouble."

"Yes, yes," cried the King somewhat testily. "I am also in

a temper occasionally and I shall soon fly into a very bad one if you talk about going away so suddenly. This unexpected news has quite upset me—dear me! This is too bad. Just stay one more day to please me. If you hurry away so suddenly the courtiers will think that we have had a quarrel or that something is wrong."

"Your Majesty surely knows by now that I would most gladly do anything to give you pleasure, but I cannot disobey my father. I must therefore say 'Good-by' now, and I once again thank you for giving me your beautiful and sweet daughter. I will take every care of her and you will hear from us in due course."

The King saw that the Prince was determined to depart. He therefore gave his consent with the best grace he could command. He gave orders for a large retinue to accompany the Princess and her husband. He told his daughter that she might take with her his court harpist and retain him as one of her attendants in her new home. Prior to his departure the Prince gave beautiful presents to all the court officials and also a large box of jewels to the King. At last the bride and bridegroom left the palace. The King stood on the balcony and waved his hand to his daughter. Every mark of honor was naturally shown to the Prince and Princess. Away the cortège went, many of the followers being afoot, the rest on horseback.

On the third day after their departure they saw in the distance a large and beautiful city. The Prince then turned to all who had followed him and said,—

"Yonder is the capital of my father's kingdom. I now wish to bid you all farewell. Return to your homes, as I do not wish to trouble you to accompany me any longer. I thank you for your courtesy in coming thus far. I appreciate your attention very much indeed."

The retinue heard these words in great surprise. They begged him to allow them to accompany him a little further.

"If we may not," said they, "come as far as the castle, let us at all events see you and our dear Princess enter the city gates. We will then return home."

"You will return now or not at all," cried the Prince with flashing eyes. "I almost feel inclined to enjoy the pleasure of doing a little evil to all of you. You are, one and all, in my power. You think that I am a Prince. I am nothing of the kind. You imagine that I am a human being. You are mightily mistaken."

"What are you then?" they cried in dismay.

"I am a demon in human shape. Were it not for the fact that you have been very courteous to me and the Princess my wife, I would not suffer you to return at all. I should keep you here in my kingdom as prisoners and slaves. I went to your lord the King to punish him for his abominable pride. He loves money more than anything else. Virtue, character and true nobility do not count in his eyes. He prefers appearances to reality—and for once in his life he has got his preference. Your King asked me my name: go and tell him that I am the son of Satan. You will not easily forget it once you have heard it. I know that my personality usually makes a great impression. I think your King and master will remember me all the days of his life. In giving the Princess to me he thought the lines of her life were being laid in pleasant places. But pleasant places are not to be bought with money. It is not all gold that glitters. The love of money is a terrible spell that casts misfortune and unhappiness upon all those who love it above all things. When people are ready to sell body and soul for gold and silver there is no hope for them. Your King has sold his daughter to the Devil and there is no hope for either of them."

When the Princess heard these terrible words she screamed in fright and fell to the earth in a dead faint. She was quickly raised up from the ground by the harpist, who was so sweet and gentle in all his ways. He led her to a tuft of grass where she could rest herself. The retainers stood still as though they were bewitched. At last one of them turned to the disguised demon and said,—

"What proof can you give us that what you say is the truth?"

"Proof, indeed!" cried he. "See!" He touched the ground with his golden sword and lo! a column of fire and smoke arose from the earth. "I will give you further proof," he added. "I now command all the jewels and gifts which I gave to the King and the officials on the day of my departure to change into tinsel and dross. You will see that this has happened when you reach the palace. Now tell me when will that be if you return at once?"

"Why, in three days, of course," said they. "Is to-day not the third day since we left the King?"

"Yes, that is correct, but you will not be able to reach your homes in three days. When I am with you the way is soon covered. As soon as you leave me it will take you three weeks to cover the same ground which took me but three days. If this should prove to be true, you need have no hesitation in telling your master all that you have seen and all that I have spoken. Now, good folk, begone! I am tired of talking and I want to take my wife to the castle without any further delay. Farewell."

The retainers had barely heard the last word when they saw the Prince and Princess, followed by the harpist, leaving them. They therefore determined to get back home as quickly as possible. They were terribly afraid and they were exceedingly glad to escape from the demon. As he had foretold they spent three weeks on their return journey.

When at last they reached their homes they heard that the King was in the greatest distress. He declared that he had been swindled. To his courtiers he said,—

"See! this box of jewels which my son-in-law gave me is not now worth a penny. It is full of imitation rubbish, tinsel not fit to be seen in my palace."

When he heard the tale of the retainers he swooned and never regained consciousness. The news that his only daughter had married a demon was too much for him. His pride was struck low. He lingered on for two days and then he died, much to the regret of his servants.

Meanwhile the demon Prince and his beautiful young

bride had reached the castle where they were to live. The town in which the castle stood was inhabited by gnomes and fairies, the subjects of King Satan. Of course there were no human beings in the town except the unfortunate Princess and her trusty harpist. The Princess had longed to ask her husband to suffer her to return to her father when he had dismissed the retinue, but she was afraid that not only would he refuse her request but that probably he would kill her on the spot. She now knew that her foolish pride had met with its just punishment. She submitted to her awful fate with a resignation born of despair. Her only solace was the company of the talented harpist, whose sweet music enchanted her and made her forget her terrible doom. Her demon husband also professed to admire the skill of the musician, saying,—

"I am a great lover of good music, and I must confess that I consider your harpist to be a real artist. I am glad you brought him with you."

Three years passed, and one day the Prince came to his wife when she was listening to the strains of the harp. He listened for awhile, and then standing up cried aloud,—

"Enough! Now, dear wife, your time to depart hence has come."

"What do you mean?" she cried with terror in her eyes.

"You must come away from this home."

"Whither must I go?"

"You must go to Hell," said he with a horrible grin on his handsome face.

The unfortunate Princess knew that to resist would be madness. She arose and said, "I am ready, lead on." Her husband went in front of her and she followed with a heavy heart. She recalled her past life and regretted her folly in refusing to listen to the many good men who had desired to win her hand. "I was blind," she murmured, "not to see the real and true men. I am now reaping the harvest of my sin. I rejected the genuine and now I have the sham."

At last they came to the grim portals of Hell, which are

never closed. He handed her over to the custody of the sleepless guardians who are ever ready to receive their unhappy victims.

"Farewell, sweet wife! You are going to the fiery furnace where not only gold and silver are tried but where hearts and souls are also tested and judged. I am sorry I cannot accompany you," he added in a harsh voice that seemed to whip her soul at every word, "but I can tell you that you will meet with strict justice. Listen, and let me prepare you for your fate. You will be in a little world where everything you touch will turn into gold. You will like that, for you love gold. The bread you would eat will become gold as soon as you put it to your mouth. The water you take to quench your thirst will change into molten gold directly you put your goblet to your lips. The fruit you grasp will become golden in your hand. Gold and gold will be your punishment for all eternity. Farewell!"

She passed within and he turned his back and left the last abode of the hopeless.

Her faithful harpist had accompanied her till she came to the portals of Hell. He then withdrew a step or two. He gazed in front of him, curious to know what Hell looked like.

"Whom do I see yonder?" he exclaimed in surprise. "Well, I am shocked to see my old friend Nathan the harpist with his harp in this terrible place. Hullo! old Nathan, what are you doing here?"

"As you see, I am playing my harp in Hell. Good friend, beware! Do not advance a step nearer, do not follow the beautiful lady who has just been admitted. If you do you will be in Hell, and once here there is no return. I will henceforth look after her and play to her whenever I am permitted to do so."

"Thanks very much for your good advice, which I shall be most careful to follow. Now be good enough to tell me, dear friend, how is it that although you are in Hell you are not burning with Hell's fire?"

"I will gladly tell you the reason why I am not burning.

When I came here I was asked by the angels of mercy, justice and righteousness, whether I could remember having done any act of justice or deed of love or work of righteousness. After much thought I could only recall one good deed in my life."

"What was that?"

"Don't be in such hurry. We are very patient here and you must give me time to tell you. My good deed was the following. I was always glad to play my harp free of charge at the weddings of the poor in order that they also might for once in their wretched lives have a happy time and enjoy their wedding festivity by means of my harp's sweet strains. This saved me and my harp from Hell's fire."

"Thanks awfully for this piece of valuable information. I shall take a leaf out of your book. Your example shall find in me an excellent follower. Tell me, good Nathan, do you really think I shall escape Hell's fire if I do as you did? Stay—I will do more. I will also give half of all my earnings to the poor. I receive good pay when I play in the houses of the rich and I can well afford to give half away. I will always be ready to play free of charge at the weddings of the poor. I will also try every day to make some one happy, for we know that the strains of the harp drive away grief and cares."

"Do all that and you will never be in Hell at all."

"Good! Now tell me, dear Nathan, how am I to find my way home: which road must I take?"

"Keep to the right and go straight forward. I am very sorry I am unable to leave this dreary place. I should be so happy to accompany you on your return to the lovely world. But it cannot be."

"Many thanks for directing me. You can do me just one more favor."

"Well, what do you want?"

"Give me some sign or token to prove that I have spoken to you. If, by the grace of God, I return to my home, I shall, of course, tell my friends of all that I have seen and heard. When I say that I saw my good friend Nathan in Hell

my audience will laugh at me and in derision they will ex-
claim: 'O yes! what a delightful fairy tale you are telling.'
When I reply that it is not a fairy tale but the sober truth
they will all cry out in chorus, 'Prove it.' Now just help me
to prove my tale."

"Very well. Stretch out the little finger of your left hand
and reach over until it is about half-an-inch in here. I will
then come as near as I can and touch it. You will immediately have all the proof you need."

"I am ready. Here we are touching one another. . . . Stop
it, please, you are burning my finger. It is not only burning, it is shining with a blue light and smells of sulphur.
Enough! I have proof, much more than I ever wished to
have! Can't you help me to get rid of the burning pain and
the shining effect? I don't like it at all."

"No, no, be satisfied. It is only the tip of your finger and
not your whole body that is on fire. Now go the way I
pointed out, and all will be well. Farewell, and don't come
back."

"Farewell."

Nathan saw his friend with his harp under his arm beginning his return journey. On and on he went, and after
wandering many days in strange lands, crossing hills and
dales, fields and deserts, he came at last to his own city.
How glad he was to reach his home! All who saw him were
astonished to see his burning and shining finger. The
harpist kept his word and played for the poor free of
charge. He gave away in charity half of his earnings. The
more he played on his harp the cooler grew his finger. At
last it became quite normal, while the music of his harp
became sweeter and sweeter till it one day charmed the
old harpist into the sweetest sleep of his long and hard
life. He still sleeps on, hearing the harmonies of love and
charity.

Maàseh Book (*Chap Book*),
ed. Rödelheim, p. 54a.

X. The Magic Leaf

ONCE upon a time there lived on the banks of the Euphrates in Babylon a holy man who spent his days and nights in the performance of religious rites and in meditation. He determined to go to the Holy Land in order to end his days in Jerusalem, where the Temple of God stood. On and on he went and at sundown he felt very tired, and sat down to rest his weary feet. He would have been glad to fall asleep but was unable to do so owing to the loud twittering of the birds overhead. He sat up watching. He saw two of the birds quarreling, while the others went on chirping for all they were worth. At last one of the two birds that were quarreling killed the other, whereupon all the rest took to flight. The holy man sat still, for he was curious to learn what would happen.

He did not have to wait very long before he saw a large bird flying towards him. The bird passed him and came near to its dead brother. In its little beak it held a small green leaf which it placed on the head of the dead bird. Immediately the leaf touched it, a wonderful miracle happened. It was re-animated and stood upon its feet. It shook its pretty feathers, flapped its wings and flew off.

The man was astounded at what he had seen. He sprang up, saying to himself,—

"I must get that magic leaf, it will enable me to quicken all the dead in the Holy Land when I arrive there. This is truly a most extraordinary slice of luck to find such a priceless treasure. I suppose this leaf comes from the tree of life in the Garden of Eden. Had I not witnessed the miracle I should never have believed it possible. This leaf is worth untold gold and will bring me good fortune and happiness."

He picked up the leaf and put it away carefully in the fold of his turban. He resolved to spend the night beneath a tree near by, as no houses were visible. Next day he awoke very early. The sun rose, scattering with his powerful beams the morning mists.

He pursued his journey after he had said his morning prayers. He had not walked many hours when he came to a farm. He was about to enter in order to ask for food, when he saw just outside the doorway a dead fox. He went up to it and said to himself,—

"Now I will get out the magic leaf and see if it will re-animate this dead fox. I like to experiment with this most wonderful leaf."

He took off his turban and took out the precious leaf, which he put on the head of the fox. No sooner had the leaf touched the fox, than the latter jumped up and ran away as quickly as his legs could carry him.

"This is marvelous," he exclaimed, while picking up the leaf, which he replaced in the fold of his turban.

He then knocked at the door of the farm-house and was admitted. He asked for a little food which was readily given him by the owner, an old farmer.

"Did you know there was a dead fox outside your door?" he asked the farmer.

The latter replied, "Of course I did, for I killed him yesterday."

The Visitor: "The fox is not there now."

Farmer: "Where is he?"

Visitor: "He ran away just before I knocked at your door."

Farmer: "That is impossible."

Visitor: "Go and look. You will not see the fox."

Farmer: "Come with me and let us look together." They went to the door, and sure enough the fox was not to be seen.

The Visitor: "I brought the dead fox back to life. I am a holy man and I can revive the dead."

Farmer: "You are a foolish chatterbox. If what you say be true, take my advice and do not meddle with the mysteries of life and death. God alone will quicken the dead. Now, farewell."

The farmer went into his house and shut the door. Whereupon the holy man went on his way, thinking that God had given him such a wonderful treasure because he had lived such a holy life.

"The old farmer does not understand the good fortune which has befallen me," he muttered.

He had not proceeded very far when he saw a dead lion in the road. He thought of testing once more the efficacy of the wonderful leaf.

"This shall be my last experiment," he said, as he took off his turban.

He then took out the magic leaf and placed it on the head of the lion. This was no sooner done than the lion arose and growled with delight at seeing a fine meal in front of him in the shape of the holy man. The next instant as the holy man began to regret his extreme folly in restoring the dead lion to life, the latter sprang upon him and devoured him. The lion also ate the magic leaf. With this disaster the possibility of reviving the dead passed away and mortals must now wait patiently for the quickening of the dead till the great day of the resurrection comes.

Eccles. Rabbah, Eccles. v. 9.

XI. The Prince and the Rabbi

IN the thirteenth century there lives a Prince in Beaudun in France. He was very narrow-minded, because he wished all his subjects to think alike. No two human beings are exactly like. The Prince had a great friend who was a Jew, learned in statecraft and diplomacy. The fact that he was a Jew and a Rabbi as well greatly vexed the Prince. "I am a Christian," said the latter one day, "and I want every one in my domains to follow my example."

"Noble Prince!" replied the Rabbi, "you cannot possibly mean what you say."

"What do you mean?" asked the Prince.

"I mean," said the Rabbi, "that you would not care to see all your subjects princes, your equals. Be glad that you have diverse subjects, Christians and Jews, nobles and peasants, bakers and tailors, and so on."

"What I really mean," said the Prince, "is that in the matter of religion I intend to have uniformity—all my subjects must be Christians. I shall order that all Jews in Beaudun be baptized on Ash-Wednesday next. A large candle shall be lit in the market-place, and every Jew who comes to the Cathedral to be baptized shall be received by Holy Church provided he comes while the candle is yet burning. All who absent themselves do so on pain of death."

Ash-Wednesday came and the large candle was solemnly lit by the Archbishop. The Cathedral doors were thrown wide open, but not a Jew came to be baptized. That same night every Jew and Jewess, man, woman, and child, except the Rabbi, had been lodged in the city prisons. They wept and prayed, for they knew that it was their last night on earth. Next morning they were led to the stake and perished amid the flames, crying with their last breath: "Hear, O Israel, the Lord is our God, the Lord is one." They thus sanctified the Holy Name of the One God, their Heavenly Father.

The Prince sent for the Rabbi and tried to persuade him to become a Christian, as his life would be forfeit if he remained a Jew. "Unless you accept baptism, I shall not be able to save your life. I am anxious to retain your friendship and your valuable services to the State, but I cannot employ a Jew. If you do as I desire, I will confer upon you the greatest honors. You shall be my daily companion and friend. Surely this is sufficient to induce you to ask the Archbishop to baptize you."

The Rabbi replied: "You know how very highly I prize your friendship and confidence. You surely realize that I would gladly give my wealth, my possessions, even my life for the welfare of the land where I live. But there is a limit which I cannot trespass, and that is the limit of honor. You promise to confer upon me the greatest honors at your command. What are the honors which a Prince of flesh and blood can confer compared to the honors which God, the King of kings, confers on His servants? Can you moreover really find any distinction which can replace that which I believe has already been bestowed on me by God?"

"What do you mean?" asks the Prince.

"I refer to the honor and distinction of being a Jew, a member of God's Kingdom of priests, one of His Holy Nation."

"Enough, Jew!" cried the Prince in a furious rage. "I will give you five minutes to make up your mind; either you become a Christian or you perish with the other Jews at the stake."

At the expiration of the five minutes the Rabbi again addressed the Prince saying: "Dear Prince! I must admit that my present intention is not to be baptized. Nevertheless, there is just a possibility that I might alter my mind if I were to see my brethren in faith, the unfortunate Jews, perishing at the stake. This horrible vision might shake my fortitude, for I am very human and weak in my spirit. To think that I might also burn at the stake might make me afraid. My fear would probably be increased if you stood at my side. Come then, let us go now together to the market-place and God in His grace may move me to act even as He may desire."

The Prince with joy on his face cried eagerly: "I quite approve; let us go."

When they came to the market-place they were told that there were no more Jews to be burnt. Now this stirred the heart of the Rabbi, and he also determined to be as brave as his heroic brethren. He went with the Prince nearer and nearer to the fire. All of a sudden he seized the Prince with both hands, for he was a very strong man, and thrust him right into the fire. He then threw himself upon him and they both perished in the flames.

Shebet Jehudah, § 35.

XII. The Princess and the Beggar

NOW King Solomon had a daughter, who was the most beautiful princess in the world. On her fifteenth birthday her wise father made up his mind to look at the stars in the heavens and to read therein the fate of his beloved child. That night he gazed at the constellations in the sky and discovered that the lovely princess was destined to become the wife of a beggar whose poverty was to be greater than that of any one in his kingdom. He also read in the stars that his daughter and her future husband would be blessed with children. King Solomon turned his eyes from the heavens in shame and anger. This outlook for his daughter's future happiness was not at all to his liking. "I wish I had not been so inquisitive," said he to himself. "Why did I try to read the future? Now I know what is her destiny I am wretched and unhappy. I will take steps to prevent such an unfortunate marriage. It's not fair that marriages should be arranged in heaven."

That same night he went to his study and rubbed his magic ring on which the Holy Name of God was engraved. Before him stood Ashmodai, King of the Genii. "Gracious Master, command and I will obey thy will."

"Listen then, Ashmodai. Near the sea-coast opposite Joppa is a small rock in the sea. I wish to have a very lofty tower built on this rock. The base of the tower must cover the entire surface of the rock except where the steps lead to the entrance."

"Before sundown to-morrow, O son of David! thy wish

shall be fulfilled." The next moment the demon had vanished.

On the next day the King sent for the beautiful princess and told her that she would in three days' time go with him to one of his castles near the sea and reside there for some time. "Thy will is my pleasure, O dearest of fathers," said the princess when she heard her father's wish. At the appointed time the King and the princess with a retinue of seventy servants set out for the port of Joppa. When they arrived there they embarked on the King's ship and sailed to the rocky shore where the tower stood. The rooms were furnished in a most princely manner. There was everything that one could wish for. Of course there was also a sufficient store of food in the tower for all the needs of the princess and her attendants. The King told the attendants that they were to watch by day and night and see to it that no stranger set foot within the tower. "As soon as the princess and you are all in the tower I will have the only door, which is at the entrance, removed and replaced by brickwork. You are to prevent any communication whatsoever reaching her. If you disobey, your lives will be forfeit." The King kissed his daughter and warned her not to try to escape. "In good time I will fetch thee and then thou shalt live in my palace on Mount Lebanon. Now farewell." She promised her father to obey and waved her hand as she saw him embark on the royal ship. "Good-by," she cried with a sad voice, standing on the roof. She did not quite like the idea of being shut up in the lonely tower.

While the King was embarking, his servants were removing the door of the tower and bricking up the doorway. It was now impossible for any one to enter or leave and the only means of exit was through a skylight on the roof.

On his journey home King Solomon smiled and said to himself: "I will now see if my plan will be a success. I think I shall for once in a while have my own way. After all this lovely girl is my child and I can surely arrange her marriage as I like. I am not satisfied with the choice of the bridegroom made by the stars. A beggar should marry the daughter of a beggar but not the daughter of a king. I shall wait and see. Whatever happens will, I hope, be for the best."

About three years later it happened that on a certain day a beggar left his home in Acco, a seaport north of Mount Carmel. He could not find even a crust of dry bread in his town and he determined to seek his fortune whithersoever his Heavenly Father might direct his steps. He had spent all his time since childhood in studying the Holy Law. His beggarly clothes were all in tatters. On and on he went, hungry and thirsty. He had no idea where he would be able to find a night's lodging. "Ah!" said he to himself, "what a funny world we are in. Rich and poor, wise and foolish, happy and unhappy people live according to the will of God. He it is who bringeth low and raiseth up, who maketh poor and maketh rich. What is my fate? God alone knows." On and on he tramped. The sun was beginning to set and the air grew cold. He then saw something that attracted his attention. It was in a field just off the highway. He went to see what it was. He found that it was the hide of an ox. "This is lucky," cried he in delight; "God has now provided me with a night's lodging. I will roll myself in this skin and escape the cold wind. I will sleep as happily as though I were in a warm cozy bed." He said his night prayers and asked God to send his good angels to watch around him and to take charge over him. In a minute he was tightly rolled up in the skin and in the twinkling of an eye he slept the sweet sleep of the weary.

The moon was shining brightly. A mountain eagle flew near by and seeing the skin rolled up mistook it for the dead body of an ox. He pounced upon it and seized it with his talons and bore it high up in the air. On and on he flew, across hill and dale, over river and sea, till he reached the tower on the rock in the sea near Joppa. He dropped the heavy hide on the roof of the tower at the break of day. The eagle flew away to his nest on the hills, intending to return later in the day with his family and to dine off the flesh of the ox which he thought was beneath the hide.

No sooner had the eagle dropped his burden than the beggar awoke and held his breath, for he knew neither where he was nor what had befallen him. Hearing the flapping of the eagle in his flight to his nest, the poor man ventured to get out of the hide to see where he was. He was more than amazed to find himself on the roof of the huge tower surrounded by the sea. He said to himself: "How shall I ever escape from this lonely place? Hark! Who's that opening the sky-light? See, here's a strange sight, the like of which I have never seen. Is it a fairy yonder? Who has ever seen such a lovely face, such eyes as blue as the sky, such hair like gold in the sunshine? It must be a fairy princess or I am still dreaming. Look, she is coming nearer and nearer to me. She is going to speak—"

"I am in the habit of taking a little exercise out here every morning before breakfast. Little did I ever expect to see a stranger here. Please excuse the liberty I take in speaking first, but this is my home. I like to know the names of all who come here. Now tell me, please, who art thou and how didst thou get here?"

"Gracious lady! I am a Jew, a student of the Holy Law of Israel. My home is in Acco, in the land ruled by the wisest of kings, Solomon. My father and mother are no longer on this earth. I am very poor and I left home yesterday to seek my bread whithersoever God might lead me. After sunset I went to sleep in a field, wrapping myself in the hide of an ox. I was so happy in my sleep, dreaming sweet dreams. All of a sudden I awoke by falling heavily on this roof. When I opened the hide and came out I saw a huge eagle flying over the sea. I am sure that this bird brought me here. Now I pray thee, good lady, forgive me for being here uninvited. Pray let me descend and depart."

"That is impossible."

"Why?"

"There is no door to this tower."

"Am I bewitched?"

"I do not think so."

"Art thou a fairy?"

"Of course not."

"Why is there no door to the tower?"

"So that no one shall enter or depart. And even if there were a door, escape is impossible. We are on a rock in the middle of the sea. Boatmen are not allowed to come near to the tower unless it be by the King's order."

"Do not look at me. I am so ashamed of my rags."

"That is easily put right. Come with me and I will show thee a nice room where new clothes are at thy disposal. There thou wilt also be able to have a good wash and make thyself comfortable. Then we will have breakfast together."

"This is all too lovely. Is it all true? Am I still dreaming?"

"Not at all."

"I am most grateful for all thy kindness. I shall be most happy to be thy guest for the present."

The princess led the beggar to the room and left him at the door, after telling where he was to find her for breakfast. When he had washed and changed his clothes he came to the princess. He was the most handsome man she had ever seen. There and then she fell in love with him. She asked him whether he would like to marry her. He at once consented. In his great joy he said to her: "I will now write out our marriage contract."

She gave him parchment and a quill, saying, "I am very sorry to tell thee that I cannot find any ink."

"That matters not. I can supply a good substitute."

"What will it be?"

"See, I will just open this little vein in my arm and with a few drops of blood I will write the deed."

He did so. Then taking her right hand he slipped on her forefinger a golden ring which his dying mother had given him and which he had on his little finger. "Behold," he cried, "with this ring do I betroth thee unto me and marry thee according to the Law of Moses and Israel, God and His angels Michael and Gabriel being our witnesses."

In time they had a sweet little daughter. News of this un-expected event was duly reported by Ashmodai to King Solomon. He at once set out to visit the princess. When he reached the rock on which the tower stood, he carefully examined the brickwork which had replaced the doorway. It had not been touched. The King now ordered his ser-vants to remove the bricks and to replace the door. He then entered the tower. All the attendants were sum-moned to meet King Solomon. They were in mortal dread, fearing that their lord would punish them with death on account of what had happened. When the King saw them he said:

"Do ye know anything about the marriage of the princess? Were ye present at the ceremony?"

"No, your gracious Majesty."

"I will go and ask the princess to tell me the truth, wait ye here till I return."

The King went to the room of the princess and after greeting her he asked her:

"Is it true that thou art married?"

"Of course, dearest father."

"Who is thy husband?"

"A noble Jew. God sent him to me. He is the most hand-some man in the kingdom. I fell in love with him at first sight. I asked him to have me for his wife. He agreed most kindly and I am glad he was good enough to fulfill my wish. I hope, father dear, that thou art come to bless our darling baby, my husband and me. My husband is a great scholar. He knows the Holy Law by heart. He is a noble and good man."

"I can see, my child, that thou dost love him."

"That indeed I do."

"Call him and let us see one another."

The princess went to fetch him. When he saw the King, he fell on his face to the ground and cried:

"Long live King Solomon!"

"I understand from my daughter here that thou art her husband."

"Even as thou sayest, O lord King."

"Hast thou a marriage contract?"

"Here it is."

"Tell me all about thy family and thy history."

When he had told the King all that he desired to know, Solomon embraced him and blessed him. He saw that this poor youth was the very man destined to be his daughter's husband. After all, marriages are made in Heaven. Solomon rejoiced when he found his son-in-law to be a learned and good man, fit to be married to the most beautiful princess in the whole world. They lived very happily all the days of their life, leaving several sons and daughters to mourn their loss when they slept into death in a ripe old age.

Tanchuma
(ed. Buber, Introduction, p. 68b).

XIII. The Castle in the Air

L ONG, long ago there lived two famous kings. One was
Pharaoh, king of Egypt. The other was Sennacherib,
king of Assyria. Pharaoh was a very warlike ruler. He had
an enormous army. His soldiers were very brave and most
skillful with their bows and battle-axes. Their King delighted to see them daily on parade in the sandy desert
near the royal palace. He watched them in summer and in
winter. His object in having his fine men constantly drilled
was to have them ready for battle, which he would have
gladly welcomed should occasion arise to wage war. He
often wished, as he rode home to his palace after drill,
that he had a palace or castle in the desert. But he knew
that the sand of the desert would never do for a foundation and therefore it was useless to build his residence
there.

One day a rumor reached him that the King of Assyria
had caused his wise Minister of State, named Achikar, to
be killed. Pharaoh had always been afraid of having a
quarrel with this man, who knew so well how to advise
his master King Sennacherib. Now that he was supposed
to be dead there was nothing to fear. Therefore Pharaoh
wrote a very rude letter to the king of Assyria as follows:
"Health be to thee. It is good for kings to pay tribute to
those who are wiser and stronger than they are. Thou
must either pay tribute to me or I must give thee tribute.
Be it known to thee that I desire to have a castle built in
the air over the desert of Egypt. I know that it is not a

very easy thing to have a castle between heaven and earth. It is very good for kings to learn how to do difficult tasks. I therefore order thee to send me within six months a clever man who is a skilled architect, that is to say, a man who can draw the plans of the castle and guide the workmen. He must also bring with him builders for the work. When thou hast sent me such men I will collect and send thee the taxes of Egypt for three years. If, however, thou shouldst neglect this my request and fail to send me such men of whom I have written above, then shalt thou collect and send me as tribute the taxes of Assyria for three years. Failing this, I will gather my mighty army and come to fight thee. I will lay waste thy land and take away thy kingdom. From thy overlord, Pharaoh, King of Egypt."

As soon as this letter reached Sennacherib, he read it and handed it to his Ministers of State. They advised him to summon all his nobles and to ask their advice, saying, "What shall we do?" He followed this plan. When the nobles had heard the letter read, they held their peace. Their silence distressed Sennacherib, who did not know what was to be done. He then called together all the old and learned men, including the star-gazers and magicians. As soon as they were all seated in the royal council room the King told them what the King of Egypt had dared to write. "How shall I act, what advice do ye give?"

"O Lord, great King!" said one of the star-gazers, "know that there is none in thy kingdom who could deal with King Pharaoh except the wise Achikar, the royal secretary. Alas! he was put to death at thy command. Why ask us to advise thee? Who is able to build a castle in the air between heaven and earth? We cannot help thee."

Now as a matter of fact it was unknown to the King Sennacherib that Achikar was not dead at all. He had been condemned to death on a false charge of betraying his king and country. On the day when he was supposed to suffer death, he had recognized in the public executioner a friend, whose life he had once saved. In return the kind-hearted friend spared his life and a condemned criminal took Achikar's place at the public execution.

When King Sennacherib found that there was no one in his kingdom to help him, he began to lament over Achikar's death. In the hearing of all his courtiers he said: "Alas for thee, noble and wise Achikar! How well didst thou manage the affairs of our kingdom! All the secrets and thoughts of men didst thou know. Woe is me for thee! how did I destroy thee. I listened to the tittle-tattle of evil men and in consequence thou art no more. Ah! who can give thee to me just for once, or bring me word that thou art alive? I would give him half of my kingdom. Moreover, I would also give him thy weight in gold."

With tears in his sad eyes the King sat on his throne of gold after he had spoken these words. Then one of the courtiers present came near to the king and said: "O king! live forever. I was the public executioner when Achikar was sentenced to death. Now command thy servants to cut off my head."

"Why should I do this?"

"O my lord! every one that doeth not the order of the king is worthy of death."

"That is right. What hast thou failed to do?"

"I have disobeyed the king's command."

"When and how?"

"Thou didst command me to put Achikar to death. I knew that one day thou wouldst repent thee concerning him. I was also aware that he had been very greatly wronged. He was, indeed, not guilty of any crime. I therefore saved his precious life and I hid him."

"Stay! I command thee. If it really be as thou sayest and thou wilt show me Achikar alive, then will I give thee great wealth and make thy rank above that of all thy friends. Thou shalt not die, but thou shalt live as the king's friend in honor and happiness. Fetch Achikar quickly and my heart will rejoice."

After a brief interval Achikar came before the astonished king and all his courtiers. When Sennacherib saw him he wept and was mightily ashamed to look him in the face. He knew that he had wronged him. He cried aloud: "Praise be to God Who hath brought thee back!"

Achikar turned to the King and said: "Because I have seen thy face, my lord, no evil is in my heart."

"Hast thou heard of the letter which I have received from Pharaoh, King of Egypt?"

"No, my lord King!"

"Read it, noble Achikar! Give me advice how to answer it."

Achikar took it from the king's hand and read it. He then said to the king: "My lord! concerning this matter which Pharaoh demands, be not anxious. I will go to Egypt and build thee a castle in the air. I will then bring back with me the three years' tribute of Egypt."

When the King Sennacherib heard Achikar's words he rejoiced very heartily. Then Achikar said: "Grant me, I beseech thee, a delay of forty days. I need time to consider this matter so as to arrange it successfully."

The King most readily agreed to this. Achikar went to his home in the country and told his huntsmen to capture two young eagles for him. When this had been done, he ordered the workers in flax to weave two strong ropes, each to be two thousand cubits long and one ell in thickness. He also caused his carpenters to make two large cages for the eagles. He then took two little lads, making them sit every day on the backs of the eagles. The feet of the birds were bound by the long ropes to prevent them flying away. After a while the lads were quite accustomed to their morning ride on the eagles. By means of the ropes the birds could be drawn down to the ground when necessary. Achikar also taught the boys to shout when high up in the air: "Bring bricks, bring clay, that we may build the king's castle up here, for we are sitting still doing nothing." After many days' training everything was in order just as Achikar desired. He went to the King's palace to tell him that he was ready to go to Pharaoh and to say "Farewell." Sennacherib embraced him and wished him a happy and prosperous journey. He then set out for Egypt, taking with him a company of soldiers, the eagles in their cages, the long ropes and the two boys.

At last he came to the land of Egypt. He went at once to visit Pharaoh in his palace. When he was brought before the king he bowed his face to the ground and said: "O my lord, O king! My master Sennacherib sends thee greetings of peace. He has read the letter written by thy Majesty and thanks thee mightily for the honor thou dost confer upon him by promising to give him three years' tribute if thy castle in the air is built. I have therefore come to Egypt, thy land, to build thee here a castle between the heavens and the earth. By the help of the Most High God and thy noble favor I will build it for thee as thou desirest. Please provide lime, stone, clay and workmen. I have brought with me from the land of Assyria skilled builders to complete thy castle."

The words of Achikar were heard by Pharaoh and his courtiers with great surprise. In fact, they could hardly believe their ears. The King gave orders to have all that Achikar demanded at once prepared and taken to that part of the desert where the royal soldiers were accustomed to drill. Thither came Achikar with his lads, the eagles and the ropes. The King and his courtiers also went there to see how the wonderful castle would be built.

Achikar let the eagles out of their cages. He tied the lads on their backs and also tied the ropes to the feet of the eagles and let them go in the air. They soared upwards, till they remained between heaven and earth. Then the boys began to shout, saying: "Bring bricks, bring clay, that we may build the King's castle in the air. We are sitting up here doing nothing."

The crowd below around the King were mightily astonished at all that they saw. They wondered what it all meant and what was going to happen. Achikar took a rod in his hand and began to beat the King's workmen who were standing still with gaping mouths, surprised beyond measure at seeing the boys on the eagles high up in the air. He shouted for Pharaoh's soldiers, saying to them: "Bring up to my skilled workmen what they require, bricks and clay. Do not hinder them from their work."

Pharaoh turned to him and said: "Tell me thy name."

"I am Achikar, the secretary of State to the King of Assyria."

"Did I not certainly hear that thy lord and king had caused thee to be slain?"

"Be that as it may. I am yet alive, for God saved me to build thy castle in the air."

"Thou art indeed mad, Achikar. Who can bring up sand, bricks and clay to thy builders up there between heaven and earth?" said the King in a temper.

"How then, my lord King! shall we build a castle in the air? I have prepared all the plans and yonder in the air are the special builders. All they need is the material. I can also tell thee this—if my lord Sennacherib, the mighty King of the Assyrian Empire, were here, he would have built several castles in the air in a single day."

"Have done with the castle, Achikar. Get thee to thy King and I will send with thee three years' tribute. Would that I had never written my foolish letter to thy lord. Give him my greetings and tell him I shall never again ask for such an impossible thing as a castle in the air. We must learn to be satisfied with such things as are possible and right. Farewell, wise Achikar."

Straightway he returned to his lord, King Sennacherib. When the news reached the King of Assyria that the trusty Achikar was returning, he went out to meet him and rejoiced over him exceedingly. When they met the King cried: "Welcome home, dear Achikar, the strength of my kingdom, the prince of my realm." Achikar told him how he had fared in Egypt, and with pride showed him the three years' tribute sent by Pharaoh. King Sennacherib was delighted and said: "Take of this tribute as much as thou dost desire."

"I desire naught but the safety of my lord the King. I am happy to know that I have been able to serve thee.

Continue to trust me and I will do all I can to help thee to increase in honor and greatness."

Achikar lived to be a very old man. To his last day Sennacherib honored and loved him as the wisest man in his kingdom.

Achikar, v–vii.

XIV. The Citizen of the World

THE Holy One gathered the dust for the creation of the first man from the four corners of the earth. The Spirit of Life asked God why did He do this. The Holy One replied: "If a man should chance to come from the East to the West, or from the West to the East or to any place on the face of the earth, and his time comes to depart from this world, then the dust of the earth which is in that place where he dies shall not say to him: 'The dust of thy body is not mine. Thou wast not born here in this land. Return to the place whence thy dust was gathered at thy birth.' It is for this reason that I have taken the dust to form man from the four corners of the earth. Every place on earth is man's home. Wheresoever he happens to be when he dies there is the resting-place for the dust of his body and there it returns to Mother-Earth." The Spirit of Life praised the Lord whose mercies are over all His works.

Chapters of Rabbi Eliezer, xi.

XV. The Snake's Thanks

THE following story was told at the court of David, King of Israel. It happened in those good times that an old man was walking along the road on a bitterly cold winter's day. He was feeble and had to support his old body upon a thick stick. On the side of the road he saw a snake, frozen with the cold. He felt very sorry to see one of God's creatures in pain. He went up to it and saw its eyes open and close. "Poor thing," said he, "it will soon die if it remain here much longer. Do we not read in God's Holy Bible that we must be merciful to all things which He has made? I will pick up the poor snake and try to revive it."

He hastened to take it up, and in order to give it a little warmth he put it under his coat close to his chest. It did not take very many minutes to warm it. The man was soon aware of the snake's recovery, for it began to coil its slimy body around him. Its pressure became gradually greater and greater till the man cried out in alarm: "Hold on! What art thou doing? Why dost thou squeeze me to death? Had it not been for my kindness and sympathy thou wouldst by now have perished on the roadside. When I picked thee up thou wast almost frozen to death. I have given thee back thy life and in return thou seekest to kill me. Is it right to return evil for good? Is this thy way of thanking those who help thee?"

"Thou art a very nice old man. But thou dost not seem to remember what I am. Tell me that first."

"Thou art a snake."

"Exactly. I am therefore quite in order in killing thee and any man. Snakes are made to kill the children of men."

"Come, Master Snake. Let us put our case before a judge and let us hear what he has to say."

"Very well, I agree to do this. Before whom shall we state our case?"

"Before the first creature that we meet on the road."

On and on they went till at last they saw an ox coming along. The old man was pleased and called out:

"Please, Master Ox, oblige this snake on my neck and me by standing here for a few minutes."

"What do ye want?"

"We wish thee to judge between us."

"What's the matter?"

"I found this snake perishing with cold. To save its life I put it on my chest under my coat."

"That was indeed most kind," said the ox.

"I then found that as soon as the snake revived it wanted to strangle me. Please decide whether that was right, and if not kindly order the snake to release its hold on me and to depart in peace."

"Now, Master Snake, what hast thou to say for thyself?"

"Yes, I admit that this good man speaks the truth. But I am quite right in trying to kill him."

"How so?"

"Because it is written in God's Book: 'I will put hatred between mankind and the serpent.'"

"Now," said the ox, "I have duly heard both sides. I find that the snake is in the right. It makes no difference that thou hast done it a good service and in return it kills thee. The world always returns evil for good. That is the way of life as far as I know it. Just see how I fare at the hands of my master. I work for him in his field from sunrise to sunset. At night I am shut up in a cold shed with a little hay and some oats for my food. My master sits in his cozy room with a lovely bright fire to warm him. He has a nice supper of fine fish and good meat. He even drinks sweet wine whereas I only get cold water. He sleeps in a clean soft bed whilst I have not even a coverlet over my back. In a year or two when I am no longer able to work in the field he will sell me to the butcher who will kill me."

These words grieved the poor old man very much. "I am not satisfied with this judge," he cried aloud.

Leaving the ox behind he went on his way with the snake coiled around his neck.

"Let us try again, if it please thee," said the snake. "We will ask the next creature that we meet. I am sure I will win the case."

"Wait and see, Master Snake. Ah! here comes thy friend the ass. We will ask him to be the judge."

"By all means."

They both told their story in turn to the ass, just as they had told the ox. The ass also quoted the same words of the Bible as the ox. After a long tale of his own sorrows at the hands of ungrateful man, the ass decided that the snake was in the right.

"See!" cried the snake, "did I not say that I should win? I shall now kill thee and know that I am doing the right thing."

"Stay, Master Snake, let us be fair. We have asked two animals to judge between us. Let us also put the case before a man. It is natural that animals should judge in thy favor, for they are thy kinsmen. Come before David, King of Israel. He is a good man and will speak as is right."

"Very good, I agree."

When they came before the King, he listened very attentively to both of them. Turning to the old man, David said: "Why hast thou not kept the Holy Law? It tells us that God has put hatred between thee and the serpent. Thou hast forgotten this and now I fear I cannot help thee."

"Ah!" cried the snake in a spiteful voice, "I am in the right."

The poor man left the King's presence with a very sad heart, for the snake was beginning to squeeze him more tightly than ever. He had now given up all hope. He feared that the snake would kill him before nightfall. On and on he wandered with a heavy step, leaning heavily on his stick. At last he felt so wretched that he sat down by the side of a well saying to himself, "I will die here and the snake may fall into the well and get drowned." He saw a handsome lad near by who came running up to him and said: "Peace be unto thee."

"Peace be also unto thee, my son."

"What aileth thee, for thy face is as white as a sheet?"

"I am nigh unto death."

"Can I fetch thee a little water?"

"Nay, dear son, many thanks. I have just left King David. Alas! he cannot save my life and I must die."

"Tell me thy trouble. Perhaps I can help thee."

The old man then told him all about the snake and showed him how it had entwined itself around his neck.

"Just wait here for a few minutes and then I will go with thee to King David. Thy case shall be retried and justice will be done. I must just stay a little while here by the well. My stick fell into it and I told my attendants to dig up the ground yonder where the source of the well lies. This will cause the water in the well to increase. My stick, of course, floats on the surface. As soon as the water rises near the top of the well I can reach it and as soon as I get it we will go to the King."

This action of the lad seemed very clever in the eyes of the old man. He therefore resolved to return with him to the King. At last they came before David. The lad, who was Solomon, the king's son, fell on his face to the ground. His father told him to rise up. He did so and kissed the king's hand.

"May I speak, dear father?"

"Speak, my son."

"Why didst thou not decide this man's case in his favor?"

"Because it serves him right to find himself in his present unfortunate state."

"How so, father dear?"

"Because he did not act according to the teaching of the Holy Law."

"O father, give me, I beseech thee, permission to sit in judgment in this case."

"Most gladly will I do so, if thou wilt be able to prove to

me that I have not done justice to this unlucky man. Come, beloved son, and sit on my chair of state. I will listen to thy words of wisdom. May the God of my fathers be with thee in judgment!"

Solomon sat on his father's chair and began to say to the snake: "Tell me, why dost thou do evil to one who has dealt kindly with thee?"

"God has commanded me to do so."

"Where?"

"In his Law."

"Dost thou agree to abide by the teaching of the Law?"

"Of course I do."

"Now at once get off this man and stand on the ground even as he does."

"Why should I?"

"Because the Holy Law demands that those who have a quarrel shall stand before the judge."[1]

"I quite agree to do this. Now wilt thou judge between me and this man." The snake uncoiled its body and placed itself beside the old man. Solomon then turned to the old man and said: "The Holy Law has also a command for thee. It tells thee that thou shalt bruise the serpent's head. Do now according to the word of thy God." The old man no sooner heard Solomon's words than he raised his stick on which he was leaning and smote the snake a deadly blow on its head. The next second it was dead. King David and his courtiers were mightily astonished at the wonderful wisdom of Solomon, whose fame soon spread throughout the land. The old man thanked the prince and the King for saving his life and went his way in peace.

Chap Book
(ed. Rödelheim, f. 43b).
See also *Tanchuma*
(ed. Buber, Introduction, p. 78b).

1. See Deut. xix. 17.

XVI. The Rebellious Waters

ON the third day of the week of creation the mighty waters covered the face of all the earth. Then the Holy
One commanded the waters to be gathered together so
that the dry land might appear. The prince of the sea
forced back the rolling waves, whereupon the mountains
and hills scattered over the surface of all the earth rose
beneath the blue sky. Now the prince of the sea brought
the waters into the deep oceans. When the waters saw
this they became proud and attempted once again to
cover the face of the earth. The prince of the sea rebuked
them and warned them not to disobey the great Creator.
They refused to listen and were about to submerge the
earth when the Holy One blamed them for being disobedient. He at once subdued them and placed them beneath
the level of the earth. In order to restrain the sea He put
the sand as their boundary. Whenever the water is
tempted to rebel and to pass over its bounds, it sees the
sand and returns to its proper place.

When the sea saw the sand for the first time it said:
"What need have I to be afraid of the sand? Is it likely that
its tiny grains can hold me in check?"

The tiny grains of sand heard these proud words of the
sea. They whispered to one another: "Let us not be frightened by the big talk of the waves. It is quite true that each
one of us is very small. What of that? If we be friendly to
one another and remain united we shall be able to do
what the good Creator intends us to do. We all know what

that is. We were made to hold the great sea in check. This we certainly shall not be able to do if we quarrel and stand apart. Then each one of us will be very easily washed away by the waves. Now let us all promise one another to remain always united. Union is strength. Then we need have no fear of the raging waters. Their roaring and foam will not frighten us."

The Holy One blessed their union and to this day the golden sand holds the proud waves in check.

Chapters of Rabbi Eliezer, v.

XVII. The Goblin and the Princess

ABOUT seventeen hundred years ago there lived a very famous Rabbi named Simeon ben Yochai. His home was in Palestine. He spent all his time in teaching the word of God to the Jews who came to listen to him. In those days the Romans were the rulers of the Holy Land, for they had conquered the Jews. At that time the Roman Emperor disliked the Jewish religion because it taught its believers that there was only one God, the great Creator of all things. The Romans did not understand this simple belief. They had ever so many gods and goddesses, a god of the sea, a god of the sky, and so on. The Emperor even believed that he was also a god. All his subjects, except the Jews, prayed to his image. He thought that the only way to make the Jews worship him and the Roman gods would be to forbid them to keep their holy ceremonies. He therefore made a law telling the Jews that they must no longer keep their Sabbath as a holy day of rest. All the other Jewish laws were also forbidden to be kept by them.

When the Jews in the Holy Land heard of the Emperor's law they were deeply grieved. In their distress they cried to God for help. They also turned to their great teacher, Rabbi Simeon ben Yochai, and begged him to go to Rome to ask the Emperor to withdraw his cruel and unjust law, so that they might worship God as their fathers had taught them to do. They knew that God had so often worked miracles on behalf of Rabbi Simeon. Had he not indeed deserved this Divine mark of favor? Did he not spend day after day in reading the Holy Word of God and in teaching its great lessons? The good Rabbi consented to go to Rome if one of the teachers, named Eleazar ben Jose, would be his companion. The latter agreed to do as Rabbi Simeon desired.

Without any delay they set out on their journey to Rome. They prayed to God for His protection and blessing. At last they reached the great city of Rome, when Rabbi Simeon said to his companion: "Let us well consider what we have to do here. First of all we must see the Emperor. Then we must try, with the help of God, to persuade him to withdraw his harsh law. Let us face our difficulties and overcome them. When we get to the palace we may not be admitted. In that case we shall not be able to do anything. Again, if we should be brought before the Emperor, how do we know that he will listen to us and consider our petition? Is it likely that he will consent to cancel his own law? To do such a thing is unheard of in mighty Rome. Well do we know how the Romans rule the world. They rule according to their own ideas and not according to the wishes of their subjects."

"True, indeed," replied Eleazar, "are thy words. Perhaps the good God will help us. Whenever Israel is in distress He also grieves with them. Their sorrows are also His. Come what may, we will present ourselves, if God will, at noon to-morrow at Cæsar's palace. The rest we will leave in the hands of our Heavenly Father. Now let us look for the Jewish quarter of this great city and find a lodging for the night."

They found what they required and sat down together to eat a very modest supper. They were alone. Suddenly they were startled to see in their room a little Goblin. It came near to Rabbi Simeon and said to him with a bow of its body: "Peace be with you, O masters of the Law. Ye know me not. My name is Ben Temalion. You will probably not believe me when I tell you why I am here. The purpose of my visit is to help you. I know you have a most difficult task to perform. I think you know that this task is almost an impossible one. Is it not so?"

"It is as thou sayest," replied Simeon.

"Do you care to employ my services?"

"I do not like to make use of thy evil power."

"Stay, Master!" cried Eleazar. "Who knows whether the Heavenly Father has not sent this goblin to help us!" Turning to the Goblin, he cried:

"Speak, Ben Temalion."

"Command me, and I will try to obey."

"Tell us how thou art able to help us."

"I have all my plans fully prepared."

"What are thy plans?"

"I cannot tell you unless you both agree to let me be of service to you."

"We agree," they both exclaimed.

"Well, my plan is as follows. Know that the mighty Cæsar here in Rome has an only daughter, whom he loves more than his own life. She is, indeed, the most beautiful princess in the world. Her mother died when she was a little girl. Perhaps on account of this fact her father never refuses to fulfill her least wish. Now I intend this very night to go to the palace."

"What for?" they cried.

"I will tell you. I propose to enter her body. The princess will at once become mad. She will continue in this sad condition as long as I am in her body. When her father learns of her terrible misfortune he will do anything to have her restored to health. You two men must play the part of physicians. Go to the palace to-morrow at noon and demand to see the Cæsar."

"The guard may refuse to admit us."

"Not so. Say that you have heard that the lovely Princess has suddenly become mad. This knowledge of a Court secret will impress the guard. You must then say that you undertake to cure the princess there and then. You will at once be admitted and taken to the presence of the Emperor."

"But I am not a physician," says Rabbi Simeon. "I have

never heard that my friend here is skilled in the art of healing."

"That matters not."

"How can we cure the princess?"

"Listen, Rabbi Simeon. I will now give thee the power of healing her disordered mind. All that thou hast to do is to go to her and whisper in her ear my name, Ben Temalion. I will then leave her body, and moreover, I will give a sign that I have done so."

"What sign wilt thou give?"

"Of course the madness will disappear. But to convince you that I have really left the body of the princess, I will cause all the glass in the palace to break in pieces."

"Now, Ben Temalion, how shall we be able to see the princess?"

"When ye come before Cæsar to cure his daughter, he will cause the girl to be brought before you. She will call for thee, Rabbi Simeon."

"Why?"

"She will fall in love with thee at first sight."

"Mad indeed will she be to do such folly. I am an old man, nearly eighty years old. My white beard is enough to frighten any girl and to make her look elsewhere for love and admiration."

"Now remember all I have said. You must ask the Emperor to reward you for healing his child by granting a petition you will present to him when the princess has been restored to health."

"To be sure, that is the object of our mission. What reward dost thou ask, Ben Temalion, for thy service?"

"To help the children of men is reward enough for a goblin. Now let us wait till to-morrow and all will be well." The next instant the goblin vanished.

Next day the two Rabbis betook themselves to the Emperor's palace and demanded to be taken to the presence of the Cæsar.

"What is your business?" asked the guard at the palace gate.

"We know that the princess is dangerously ill. In fact she has lost her reason in the last twenty-four hours."

"How do you know this?"

"Never mind how. We *do* know it. Do not waste precious time. We have come to heal the Princess. We are physicians staying overnight in this city. Now wilt thou lead us to the Emperor's presence?"

"Wait here, and I will have your message sent to my mighty lord, the Emperor."

After a brief delay the order came to admit the two strangers. When the Emperor saw the Rabbis he cried in a voice full of contempt: "How now! Do ye Jews dare to enter our palace and to come before our divine presence? Think ye that ye can work miracles better than the Roman physicians?"

"Tell us, mighty Cæsar, have the imperial physicians been able to cure the beautiful princess?"

"Thus far they have not been successful."

"We shall be successful even this very day. Know indeed that life and death are not in the hands of man, but only in the power of God in whom we believe. He has sent us, this is our belief, to heal the princess. Was not your Majesty's daughter so happy and well but yesterday? Was she not like a ray of warm sunshine on a cold winter's day? Did she not rejoice your heart with her bright and cheery smile?"

"Ye speak truly indeed. Come now, what do you demand as your reward if ye heal my beloved child?"

"Grant but one petition which we will put before your Majesty."

"I swear by all the gods to do this. Know ye that the oath of a Roman Emperor is never broken."

"So let it be according to your imperial word," said Rabbi Simeon.

"Stay. Mark ye well, ye wise men of Israel, if ye fail to heal my daughter, ye shall be thrown this very day into the arena. The famished lions will enjoy their meal when they devour your bodies."

"We hear your Majesty's warning. Have no fear. We will heal the sweet princess. Now let us see Her Imperial Highness, if it please your Majesty; otherwise of course we cannot cure her."

"Let the princess be brought before us at once," cried the Emperor.

After a few minutes had passed, she was brought before her father and the Rabbis. She was deadly pale and seemed to be terribly frightened. Her eyes were staring at the two strangers. Then she stretched out her hands towards Rabbi Simeon and in an excited voice cried aloud: "Happy am I to see thee at last, O my beloved! Of thee did I dream last night. Come quickly and save me, for I am nigh unto death's door."

"Hush! my beloved child," said the distressed Emperor with deep emotion. "Come to me and take my hand."

"Go away, I know thee not, O stranger!"

"I am thy father."

"I say I know thee not. Never have I seen thee before."

"Speak not thus, dearest child."

"I want to go to my beloved yonder. He is mine and I am his."

Rabbi Simeon gave the Emperor a knowing wink and went close to the princess. He laid his hand very gently on her arm and whispered in her ear the magic name "Ben Temalion." The spell was broken. She was once again the smiling princess. Turning to the Emperor she cried in a happy voice: "O dearest Father, how glad I am to see thy face. I have had a most horrible nightmare. I have only just awoke. Who are these venerable old men? Where do they come from and why are they here?"

Before the Emperor could speak there was a terrific crash. Every piece of glass in the palace was smashed into atoms.

"What is that?" cried the Emperor in alarm.

The imperial servants ran hither and thither. They seemed to be dazed, fearing some fresh surprise. They came to the Emperor and said: "There is no one to be seen."

"Never mind," said the Emperor, "about the glass. It will be replaced. Now let us rejoice. My happiness in seeing my darling daughter restored to health knows no bounds." Turning to the princess he said: "These learned men have cured thee. I am now about to grant them any petition they may desire to make."

"I also," said the princess, "will give them precious jewels."

"Nay, gracious princess!" cried the Rabbis, "we will only accept thy noble father's favor. We ask for neither gold nor gems. We seek neither honor nor worldly goods."

"What do ye then require?"

"As your Majesty knows, we are Jews from the imperial province of Palestine. Your Majesty has recently issued a law prohibiting the observance of the Sabbath, Festivals and other sacred rites of the Jewish religion. We desire to serve our God in our own way. If we are true to God we will also be loyal to Cæsar, for it is God who raises up kings to rule the children of men. We teach our people to fear God and the King. We now put our petition before your Majesty; it is this—pray cancel the imperial law dealing with the Jewish observances."

"I have promised to grant your petition. Ye have done your part in restoring my dear daughter's health. I will at once do my share by ordering the law to which ye have referred to be canceled. Go back to your brethren in Palestine and tell them that as long as I live I will give them my favor and protection. Farewell."

With bowed heads the two Rabbis withdrew. Their hearts were full of gratitude to their Heavenly Father for His love and mercy.

Babylonian Talmud, Mecilah, 17b.

XVIII. Iron and the Trees

ON the same day when the Holy One formed the trees He also made iron and other metals. Now the trees were very proud to find that they were taller than any creatures made by God. They looked at the hills and mountains and said: "They are of course very big, but we shall grow taller and taller and one day we shall be able to look down upon them." The cedars even boasted saying: "We shall soon grow as high as the heavens and our roots will stretch from one end of the earth to the other. Then shall we be kings of the earth."

At that moment the Spirit of Meekness passed by and heard the foolish boast of the trees. In a very gentle voice the Spirit said to the cedars:

"Why don't you look at your roots; do you know what is hidden beneath them?"

"No. We cannot see what is hidden deep down in the earth. Our heads are too high up in the sky."

"Well, just let me look for you. Shall I tell you what I see?"

"Please do look and tell us what is hidden beneath our roots."

"I see a lot of metal ore, called iron."

"Why dost thou tell us about the iron metal? It is not in our way the least bit."

"No, it is not in your way now."

"Why then bother about it?"

"Listen, ye cedars and all ye trees! In days to come men

will dig in the earth and find the iron ore. They will use it for very many purposes. They will make ax-heads and then you will remember my words."

"What will then happen to us?"

"If men get wood for the handle of the ax they will cut down your fine tall trees."

When the trees heard this they began to tremble and to weep.

The Spirit asked: "Why do ye weep?"

"We are afraid."

"Why are ye afraid?"

"Because now we see that thou art right. The iron at our roots will one day cut down our tall trunks which will then lie in shame on the earth. We shall never reach the sky and we shall never be kings at all. People will burn our wood in the fire once we are cut down."

"Have no fear, ye trees! All the trouble ye foresee need not arise if ye desire to prevent it."

"How so?"

"Let none of your wood be put into the iron to make the handle of the ax and then not one of you will be touched."

Genesis Rabbah, v. 9.

XIX. David and the Insects

IT happened one day that David the son of Jesse was sitting in the lovely garden of his father's house in Bethle-
hem, not far from Jerusalem. He was resting after a long
day's hard work. He loved to gaze at the beautiful flowers
painted with the golden tints of the setting sun. Their
sweet perfume also made his heart glad and he felt so
happy to be alive in such a glorious world. Hark! The
pretty birds were singing so grandly. They were surely
praising God. He also would join in their song of praise,
thanking the great Creator for having made this perfect
world with its countless beautiful things.

His happy thoughts were suddenly disturbed by seeing
a large wasp attacking a spider. The latter had woven its
web between two twigs of a rose-bush near by. At that moment one of Jesse's servants who was ofttimes mad came
along with a large stick in his hand. As soon as he saw the
wasp stinging the unfortunate spider he drove them away
by striking at them with his stick. He then went his way,
knocking off the heads of the little daisies and buttercups
along his path.

"Well, I never," cried David in surprise, "thought that
the world was as funny as I now see it is. I was delighted
but a minute or two before with all the wonderful and
beautiful things made by God. Now I find that in this
lovely world there are also such useless creatures as I
have just seen. What earthly use is there in a madman
who knows not what he is doing, ever bent on destroying

whatever he sees? O Lord of the Universe! Tell me, I beseech Thee, why hast thou created wasps and spiders? The wasp eats honey and destroys the spiders. Of what use is it? It is not good for anything except to breed maggots. As for the spider, it spins all the year round and never garbs itself with its fine web it has woven."

The Holy One, blessed be He, answered saying:

"O David! Why dost thou despise the little creatures which I have made for the welfare of the world. An occasion will surely arise when thou wilt have great need of their wonderful help. Then indeed wilt thou know why they have been created by Me. Everything in My universe has its great purpose; even the madman whom thou mockest has also his part to play. Despise naught in the world. I love all things that are the work of My hand. I hate none of the things which I have made. I spare all things because they are Mine. To everything there is a time and a place. All My creatures praise Me."

David heard no more, for the Divine voice grew silent. There was a hush. The sun had set and the golden tints vanished. The cool wind of the twilight reminded David that it was time to get back to his father's flock and to secure the sheep for the night.

Years passed by. David was no longer the shepherd of Jesse's flock. He was now the champion of Israel. His wonderful victory over the giant Goliath made him the hero and favorite of the people. He was now the King's son-in-law, for he had married the daughter of King Saul. The princess was his reward for slaying the mighty giant. Unfortunately David's popularity brought him the envy of King Saul. At last the King sought to kill poor David. To save his life he was forced to escape and hide in the mountains. Saul and his men followed in pursuit. David was finally forced to take refuge in a small cave. "Alas!" he cried, "my enemy will now surely find me and slay me. Help me, O God! save my life."

The Holy One, blessed be He, heard his prayer and sent a spider to weave its web across the mouth of the cave.

Later when Saul and his followers came along the latter saw the spider's web. They pointed it out to the King, who said: "Truly no man has entered this cave, for had he done so he would have rent the web. Let us not waste our precious time here, but rather let us hurry along the road where we may overtake our enemy."

When they had departed David came forth from the cave. He saw the little spider hanging to part of its broken web. He took it in his hand very gently and caressed it, saying to it: "Blessed is thy Creator and thou also art blessed." He then praised the Heavenly Father, exclaiming: "Lord of the Universe! Who can do according to Thy works and according to Thy mighty deeds? Verily all Thy works and deeds are wonderful."

David then continued his flight and went on his way until he came to the land of the Philistines. He thought that he would be quite safe there. At all events, Saul would leave him alone. Now the king of the Philistines, Achish by name, was a good and pious man. As soon as David's presence in his land was discovered, he ordered his servants to bring the Hebrew hero before him. He greeted him kindly and asked him why he had run the risk of venturing into the territory of the Philistines.

"I ventured to come here for I am not safe in the land of Israel."

"Thou art mad. Thou hast saved Israel. Had it not been for thee all thy people with King Saul would now be our slaves. Dost thou tell us that thy life is not safe in thine own land?"

"O lord King! It is even as I have spoken. I am persecuted by King Saul. He seeks my life and I am safer here than in the Holy Land."

"Why does Saul persecute thee?"

"Because I slew Goliath."

It happened that the brothers of Goliath were the bodyguard of King Achish. They told the king that David was worthy of death for having slain their brother. Achish asked them:

"Did he not kill Goliath in a fair combat?"

"Have a care, your Majesty! David is entitled then to be the ruler of all the Philistines. Did not Goliath boast that if he slew the Hebrew champion the children of Israel were to be the slaves of the Philistines, and vice versa?"

David now saw that he was in a very dangerous position. It was almost certain that the brothers of Goliath would kill him if he remained in their land. How could he escape? All of a sudden the idea flashed through his mind that he might escape death if he pretended to be a madman. They might pity him and spare his life. He sat down on the steps of the palace and began to scribble in the dust. He also entirely changed his behavior. This strange conduct puzzled the Philistines.

Now King Achish happened to have a most beautiful daughter who was unfortunately mad. When he saw David's foolish pranks he said to his body-guard: "Why do ye mock me? Is it because my dear daughter is mad that ye think I like to see idiots? Is it for this reason that ye have brought before me this raving madman? Do I then lack lunatics in my kingdom? Send him back to his friend, King Saul. I have no need of such a hero."

The body-guard told David to go away. He went away with a merry heart. He thanked God that he had been fortunate enough to escape from the power of the brothers of Goliath. "Now I know," cried he, "that even a madman has a useful part to play in this most wonderful world."

When he came back to the Holy Land, King Saul gave him no rest. He was forced to live the wretched life of a fugitive. On one occasion God delivered his enemy into his hand. He chanced to enter a large cave where he found King Saul and his attendants asleep. At the entrance sat the giant Abner also fast asleep. David and his followers had to be very careful how they entered. Fortunately the legs of Abner were drawn up. David's followers urged him to kill his enemy, now that he had the chance. This he refused to do. "I will return good for evil," cried he. To prove to the King that his life had been spared, David cut off a piece of the King's robe and took hold of his cruse of water. David's men went out and he followed. They had all left the cave except David, who found himself caught beneath Abner's huge legs. The giant had just stretched himself as David wished to get out of the cave. "Dear me!" said David to himself, "Abner's legs are like two massive pillars and I am now caught between them as in a trap. O Lord! save me and answer me. My God, my God, why hast Thou forsaken me?"

The Lord heard his cry. At that moment the Holy One, blessed be He, worked a miracle by sending there and then a wasp to sting Abner. The pain caused the giant in his sleep to pull up his legs sharply. Thus David was released. He skipped over the feet of Abner and escaped. At once he praised God for His mercy in creating wasps. Never again did he have any doubt of God's wisdom in creating insects, which at first had seemed to him to be useless and even harmful. Never should we despise anything which seemed worthy to be created by the Holy One, blessed be He.

Alphabet of Ben Sira, pp. 24f.

XX. The First Vineyard

ON the same day when old Father Noah came out of the
Ark, he found close to the spot where it rested a large
vine. It had been carried away from the Garden of Eden by
the rain which came with the Flood. The vine still had its
clusters of grapes and its roots. Noah tasted the grapes
and rejoiced in his heart whilst eating the wonderful fruit.
"This is so lovely," cried he in delight, "I will plant a vineyard and have plenty of grapes and golden wine." He
found a fine hill for his vineyard and began to plant the
roots. After an hour's work he rested a while. He saw a
strange-looking fellow coming along the road and when he
came to the hill he called aloud:

"Good-morning, Father Noah, what art thou doing?"

"First tell me, whence comest thou?"

"From walking up and down the earth."

"How didst thou escape the Flood?"

"I was in the Holy Land, where the waters of the Flood
did not come."

"Thou dost ask what am I doing. I am planting a vineyard."

"What dost thou expect to get therefrom?"

"Why, grapes, of course. Out of the grapes I shall get
wine which makes the heart merry."

"Come, Father Noah, this hill is very large. Let me also
help thee in thy work and we will become partners of the
vineyard. Thou art old and thy sons do not help thee. Thou
wilt be glad of my help, for I know how to plant a vineyard."

"That's more than I do."

"So I can see."

"Very well, I agree."

The stranger was none other than Satan. He left Noah for a few minutes and when he returned he brought with him a lamb. He killed it beneath the vine which Noah had planted. He then went away and brought back a lion. He slew it also beneath the vine. He then fetched a swine and killed it. Finally he brought an ape and slew it also. He mixed the blood of these four animals and poured it over the ground of the vineyard. Meanwhile Father Noah was looking on with surprise. He turned to his partner and asked:

"Why hast thou done this strange performance? What does it all mean?"

"What I have done points to the different effects which wine has upon all who drink it."

"Please explain. I do not understand thy meaning."

"Before a man drinks wine he is like a lamb, without evil desire. He is harmless and tame. Now let a man drink one glass of good wine. He feels strong like a lion and thinks that there is no man on all the earth like himself. Now let this man take a second glass of wine. What then? He has taken more than he ought to have done. He is then like a swine in the mire. If then he take a third glass he will become drunk. He then behaves like the ape. He jumps about and dances, he plays the fool and speaks nonsense. In fact he does not know what he is doing. Dost thou understand, Father Noah?"

"I hear what thou sayest and shall bear it well in mind."

Noah and Satan then went their different ways. Noah is long dead, nevertheless Satan continues to be the partner of every one who plants a vineyard to this day.

Tanchuma, Noah, §13.

XXI. Abraham's Tree

FROM the time when the Holy One told Abraham to leave his father's house in Ur of the Chaldees, he planted the seed of a tree in every place where he stayed. In vain was all his labor. The seed never took root and nothing grew. At last he came to the Holy Land. Here also he planted the seed, and strange to say, not only did the seed take root but the most beautiful tree ever seen by men grew in Abraham's garden. Its green foliage was the talk of the land. Never before had such leaves been seen. Nor was this all. The fruit of this tree was the sweetest ever tasted. Moreover its blossoms and fruit were to be seen in summer and winter alike.

Abraham made it known throughout the land that this wonderful tree was for the benefit of all the children of men. When the weary traveler, scorched by the glare of the sun, came to sit beneath the boughs of Abraham's tree, he immediately felt refreshed. The shade cast by the tree was as cool as a mountain stream. The fragrance of the fruit was so marvelous that the thirsty and hungry who came near to it needed neither drink nor food. This was the good fortune of all who believed in God. If, however, some one came near the tree and refused to believe in the Holy One, the wonderful tree seemed to be about to wither. The shade was no longer cool, the fragrance ceased to be refreshing. Then Abraham would come and teach the disbeliever that there was one God in Heaven and on earth, ever near to all who seek Him in truth. When at last the guest of Abraham had found the truth and looked up to the heavens with faith in his heart, lo! the tree was beautiful again in all its glory. The birds hastened to sit on its branches and to join in the hymn of praise to the Lord of the world.

Jalkub Chadash, 14a.

XXII. Joseph, the Sabbath Lover

IN Ascalon in the Holy Land there once lived a poor peddler named Joseph. His greatest pleasure was to keep the Sabbath Day holy. He was a good Jew, loving God and man. The precepts of the Law were his delight and by them did he live. He was not ashamed of his religion. In fact he was very proud of being a Jew. He had a neighbor who was a heathen, very wealthy and selfish. They often met and conversed with one another. This was especially the case on Saturday when Joseph abstained from his business. They would talk about religion, especially about the Sabbath. Joseph would dwell on the value of the Holy Day, pointing out that of all the gifts bestowed by God upon humanity the most precious was the weekly day of rest. Man is not a mere machine, he needs rest and recreation. To those who observe the Sabbath and call it a delight, its weekly advent is like the arrival of a dear and intimate friend.

Joseph was wont to put by part of his daily earnings in order to spend the Sabbath Day in a festive manner. He often would stint himself and forego necessities on week days so as to have better garments than his working clothes for the Sabbath and a fine spread of food on his table in order to pay honor to the Sabbath. The poor were always welcome guests at his table on Friday nights and Saturdays. He not only honored the Sabbath, he also sanctified it. People called him "Mokir Shabbe," Sabbath Lover. He seemed to forget all his cares and troubles as soon as

the Sabbath came. He never omitted to have a spotless
white table cloth spread over his table. Then there was
the Sabbath light burning in a beautiful silver lamp. Fresh
bread and sweet wine were at hand for the Kiddush or
Sanctification. Meat and fish were abundantly provided.
Joseph imagined himself to be a king and his fancy turned
the Sabbath into a lovely princess, his bride. "Welcome!
Queen Sabbath," he cried, "come, my beloved." What a
delight it must have been to hear the Sabbath hymns sung
at Joseph's table. He and his guests thanked their Heavenly Father for the Holy Day, the day of peace and repose.
A gracious gift it was, leading the children of men to their
Father in Heaven. It is a day for man whereby he can rise
above material things and see something of the Divine
vision.

One Sabbath Day the heathen neighbor, who was a
miser, lacking nothing in the way of worldly material
things, reproached the Jew for keeping his Sabbath. "How
could any one," said he, "waste a valuable day by ab-
staining from work? No wonder you are poor. See, I am
rich and possess more than I need. I am not only prosperous but I am also happy, for my motto is 'Live to-day and
let to-morrow take care of itself.' You, and I suppose all
the Jews are like you, think otherwise. You slave all the
week for the sake of your Sabbath Day. I know you are
kindhearted. Personally I don't believe in that sort of
thing. I daresay you judge me to be callous and cold-
hearted, without any love for the poor. I certainly despise
the poor, for it is generally their own fault if they do not
get on in life. They are idle, foolish and careless."

"Good neighbor," replied Joseph, "I do not quite see the
point of your lengthy remarks. You begin by blaming me
for keeping the Sabbath Day holy, and you then say that
because I do this I am poor. You are rich because you
do not keep the Sabbath. Now I admit that I am a poor
man, but what of that? I am as happy to-day as a king. I
have feasted well and I am resting. What more could I desire? You seem to think that the only pleasure in life is

hoarding money. I differ and believe the best pleasures can be obtained when we spend money in a wise and good way. Perhaps you will always be rich and perhaps I shall always be poor, but if the question were asked: 'Who is the happier of the two?' I doubt whether you would be the one. Good-day, my friend! I must attend Synagogue for Sabbath prayer."

Joseph went his way trusting in God and loving to do His holy will, well knowing that the Sabbath was more precious than all the money in the world. "No man liveth by bread alone," thought he. Whilst Joseph was in the Synagogue his neighbor had fallen in with a brother heathen who was well known in Ascalon as a famous astrologer. They greeted one another and Joseph's neighbor asked him: "What dost thou read in the stars?"

"I read that thy fortune is on the wane."

"What dost thou mean?"

"Thy wealth will pass from thine hand to the hand of thy neighbor. This will happen within thirty days."

"Dost thou know why this must be?"

"Well do I know. The gods are very fickle in dealing with wealth. The poor man of to-day may be the rich man of the morrow. What use dost thou make of thy enormous fortune? I fear thou dost neither enjoy its benefits now nor wilt thou do so in the future. Tell me, who is thy neighbor?"

"Joseph the Sabbath lover, a Jew very poor and industrious."

"Of him have I heard. He will, so the stars seem to indicate, own all thy wealth."

"Here is a silver coin for thy evil prognostication. I fervently hope it will not come true. Now, farewell." They parted and went in opposite directions.

Fear took hold of the miser, and as he sat in his room that night staring at his gold and silver he cried: "Never shall the Jew Joseph have this money. I could not bear to see him rich and proud—and I should be poor. Horrible thought. It shall not be. I will defy fate and prevent my fortune going to the beggar Jew. He is a mean hypocrite; he deserves to be poor all the days of his life. I told him so this morning and now I am told that he is to have my money. This is ridiculous and far-fetched. The old Jew would say if he could read my thoughts: 'Man proposes but God disposes.' Well, I am going to propose and also dispose. Without delay I shall to-morrow sell all my property and buy precious pearls. I shall then leave Ascalon for good and settle in the fair lands of Italy."

Next day the miser converted all his wealth into a number of very beautiful pearls. He had them strung on a silken cord which he sewed on to his turban. That same day he left Ascalon and boarded a boat leaving the port for foreign parts. "I shall soon forget all about Joseph and the foolish astrologer," said he whilst walking on deck. At that moment a gale arose and his turban was lifted off his head and carried out to sea. At one fell blow all his fortune was gone forever. He cried and tore his hair out of his head, but all in vain. He was now a beggar.

Meanwhile Joseph was leading his usual life. On the next Friday he went, as was his wont, to purchase the best food for the Sabbath meals. He came to the fish-market and saw a very large turbot on the dealer's counter. Its price was very high and there was no one who would buy it. As soon as Joseph saw it he gave the full price without any discussion. In fact he felt very happy, for he did not remember ever having seen such a large fish. "It will not be wasted," he said to himself; "the poor will help me to consume it." He thought that it would be a sin to eat such a splendid fish on a weekday, but for the Sabbath nothing was too good. He hurried home in intense happiness and gave it with a happy smile to his dear wife. "Here, my love, we have a fish fit for a king," said he. "Yes, it shall be for a king, for you, dear husband." He kissed his wife and went to his bedroom to change his garments and to prepare himself for the Sabbath. He had barely reached the bedroom when he heard his wife's voice calling: "Come, dear Joseph, come quickly."

He hastened to her side and asked her: "Why have you called me back?"

"Look, Joseph, see what I have found inside this turbot."

"It is a string of lovely pearls," he cried in delight.

"What a lucky fish!" she said.

He rubbed his eyes to make sure that he was not dreaming.

"See, my love! God has blessed us. He has given us wealth and we shall no longer slave during the six days of toil."

"Did you hear anything about our heathen neighbor with whom you were speaking on Sabbath last?"

"I heard that he had left Ascalon after having sold all his property here. I have also heard a rumor that he bought pearls with his money. How do we know whether these very pearls of our neighbor are not the same you have taken out of the fish?"

"It matters not, good Joseph, to whom they formerly belonged. It is quite evident that God in His love has sent this fortune to us. We shall know how to use His gifts even as we know how to love and appreciate His gift of the holy Sabbath."

Babylonian Talmud, Sabbath 119a.

XXIII. The Magic Sword of Kenaz

AFTER the death of Joshua, the son of Nun, the children of Israel had peace in their land for some time. Their leader and judge was Kenaz, the son of Caleb. He was a very brave man even as his father before him. Joshua and Caleb were two of the twelve spies sent by Moses to spy out the land of Canaan. They alone gave a truthful report, while the other ten spies frightened the people by telling them that they would never be able to conquer the Holy Land. They told the people of all they had seen, especially about the cities with walls up to the sky. They also spoke of the giants who would think that the Israelites were but tiny grasshoppers. Joshua and Caleb told their brethren not to listen to this false report, for the Canaanites were faint-hearted. As a reward for being truthful Joshua and Caleb were the only two of the spies who lived to enter the promised land of Canaan.

After the death of Moses, Joshua in his turn also sent two men to spy out Jericho before he attempted to capture it. The two spies were Kenaz and his brother. When Joshua died the people chose Kenaz as their judge and ruler. The peace of the land did not last long. The Amorites, a fierce tribe of Canaan, came to attack the Israelites. Kenaz armed his people to fight against the foe. He gave an Army order that his men were to begin the attack on the morrow. He noticed, however, that a score of his men began to grumble, saying: "Lo! to-morrow when we go forth to battle our leader Kenaz will stay at home and enjoy himself. Is it fair that he should send us to fight the mighty Amorites who will kill us to a man?"

The words pained Kenaz very much. He made up his mind to teach them a lesson which they would never forget. He sent for his chief captain to whom he gave a new order, saying: "Let three hundred of my servants and as many horses be chosen to go with me this night on a secret expedition. Let only such men be taken who really desire to serve under me for the love of adventure. Let them meet me at sunset outside my tent. Moreover, let no man of the people know of this matter. Only when I am ready to start will I tell thee. Therefore go now and prepare my men that they be ready in time."

"Thy order, O Kenaz, shall be obeyed," said the captain in retiring.

He then sent spies to see what the Amorites were doing. The spies went and saw the enemy moving among the hills so as to come and fight against Israel. The spies returned and told him all that they had seen. At sunset Kenaz left his tent and went away at the head of his three hundred horsemen. In his hand he held his magic sword. All who saw it trembled like a leaf when moved by the wind. At his side he carried a trumpet. When he was about a mile from the camp of the Amorites, he turned round to his followers and said to them: "Abide ye here and I will go alone and view the camp of the enemy. As soon as I blow with my trumpet ye shall come to help me, but if I do not sound the alarm wait ye here for me."

Away he went. It was almost night and he turned his heart and thoughts to God, praying: "O Lord! God of our fathers! I beseech Thee, do a miracle now. Let me, Thy servant, be chosen to defeat the enemy. With Thy help one man can defeat a million. Then will I be able to teach Israel and all men that the Lord delivereth neither by the number of men nor by the strength of horsemen, but by Thy power. Let it come to pass when I draw my sword that it shall glitter and send forth sparks in the eyes of the Amorites who refuse to worship Thee as the only true God. Let it also be a sign unto me that Thy spirit is on me, so that when the Amorites see me they will say 'It is Kenaz.' Be with me, O Lord, and save Thy people."

At last he reached the camp of the enemy and he heard them saying to one another: "Let us arise this very night and attack the Israelites unawares. Our gods will surely deliver them into our hands." Then Kenaz felt the spirit of God coming upon him and he drew his sword out of its scabbard. When the light of it shone upon the Amorites like lightning and sparks, the terrified foes cried out: "Is not this the magic sword of Kenaz which hath slain so many of the Canaanites? Now unless we arise to kill him he will slay us. Let every one gird on his sword and begin the battle. See, he is alone."

Kenaz rejoiced when he heard these words, for he knew now that God was with him. The spirit of the Lord was like armor around his body. Without fear he went into the camp of the enemy and began to smite them. As soon as they saw his sword they trembled and fell on their faces to the ground. To help him God sent two invisible angels who went before him. One, named Gethel, smote the Amorites with blindness so that they began to kill one another, thinking that they were smiting their enemies. The other angel Zernel bare up the arms of Kenaz, for his strength was beginning to fail him. He smote forty-five thousand men and they themselves smote about the same number among themselves. When he saw that he had slain so many he wished to end the battle. He tried to loosen his hand from his wonderful sword but he could not, for its handle clave to his palm. His right hand had taken unto it the strength of the sword.

The few Amorites that had not been killed fled into the mountains. Now Kenaz wished to find out how he might loose his hand from his sword. He looked about him and saw one of the enemy running away. He pursued and caught him. He said to him: "I know that the Amorites are very cunning. Now I will let thee go and spare thy life if thou wilt show me how I may loose my hand from this sword."

"That indeed I can do. Go and take a man of the Hebrews and kill him. While his blood is yet warm hold thine hand with the sword beneath it and receive his blood on thine hand; so shall it be loosed."

"As the Lord liveth, if thou hadst said, 'Take a man of the Amorites,' I would have done so and saved thee alive. Since, however, thou hast said, Take a man of the Hebrews, that thou mightest show thine hatred, thy mouth shall be thy judge. As thou hast said, so will I do unto thee."

When he had thus spoken he slew the Amorite, and while his blood was yet warm he held his hand holding the sword beneath and received it thereon. The next moment it was loosed. Kenaz said to himself: "Surely the blood of one man is as good as that of another. What the blood of the Hebrew was supposed to do has now been done by the blood of the Amorite."

The warrior now sheathed his magic sword and returned to his men. On the way he saw a stream. Quickly putting off his garments he dived into the water and washed his weary body. The cool stream refreshed him and he came out feeling quite strong and well. He dressed and hurried along to find his troops.

Now when Kenaz had gone down alone to fight the Amorites an angel had cast upon his three hundred horsemen a heavy sleep. They slept soundly and knew not anything of all that Kenaz had done. Finding them on his return fast asleep, he put his trumpet to his lips and blew a loud blast. In a second the horsemen awoke. They stared at him with wondering eyes for they were mightily surprised to see the first streaks of dawn. "What of the night?" they asked one another.

"Tell us, O Kenaz, what happened during the past night?" they cried.

"Come ye with me and see with your own eyes what God has done for us through my hand."

He led on and they followed him. When they came to the camp of the Amorites, lo! the ground was covered with thousands of dead bodies. The horsemen of Kenaz were greatly astonished at what they saw and looked every man on his neighbor. Their leader saw their surprise and asked them:

"Why do ye marvel? Are then the ways of God as the ways of men? With man a large number is a matter of importance, but with God numbers do not count. If God willed to give victory unto Israel through me His servant, wherefore marvel ye? Now arise and let us go home to our brethren."

When all Israel heard of the mighty victory gained during the night, all the people came out to meet Kenaz and his horsemen. When they saw him they said: "Blessed be the Lord who hath made thee ruler over His people and hath shown that He can save by the hands of the few and defeat the many."

Kenaz said unto them: "Ask now your brethren here with me and let them tell you how greatly they helped to win the victory."

Then his horsemen cried aloud: "As the Lord liveth, we fought not, neither knew we anything of what Kenaz did, for we all fell asleep and we did not awake till we heard his trumpet blast at dawn this day. He then led us to the camp of the Amorites. We could hardly believe our eyes when we saw a wonderful sight. We seemed to be dreaming and we rubbed our eyes to make sure that we were really awake."

"What did ye see?" asked the people.

"We saw the ground covered with tens of thousands of slain Amorites."

When the people heard this wonderful tale they began to marvel how it all happened. At last they said: "Now know we indeed that when the mighty God wisheth to give victory He hath no need of a multitude but only of holiness and trust in Him. Alas! it was very wrong of some of us to have grumbled yesterday, speaking evil against

Kenaz, saying that on the day of battle he would stay at home whilst he sent the people to be slain in battle. We have stayed at home whilst he alone risked his life last night in going to battle. Now are we ashamed of all those who spoke slander. Let them be punished according to the law."

Kenaz hearkened unto them and did unto the men who had spoken evil words against him even as the people had demanded. He ruled over Israel fifty and four years and there was a mighty fear upon all his enemies all his days.

Biblical Antiquities of Philo, xxvii.

THE END